Other fun and informative products from Tyndale House:

101 Fun Bible Word Searches

101 Fun Bible Crosswords

The Complete Book of Bible Trivia

Willmington's Book of Bible Lists

Humor Is Tremendous

The Bible Game

People and Places in the Book Game

Distributed by:

**CHOICE ▥▬
BOOKS** of Chambersburg

Write or call:
3920 Scar Hill Road
Greencastle, PA 17225
Phone: (717) 597-4681

Your comments or questions are appreciated

74 MORE

Fun & Challenging

BIBLE CROSSWORDS

LIVING BOOKS ®
Tyndale House Publishers, Inc.
Wheaton, Illinois

Puzzles designed and created by Terry Hall, Media
Ministries, 516 E. Wakeman Ave., Wheaton, Illinois
60187-3670.

Some crossword puzzles in this book were
previously published in *365 Bible Crosswords and
Word Searches 1992 Calendar.*

Unless otherwise indicated, Bible references are
from *The Living Bible,* © 1971 owned by assignment
by KNT Charitable Trust. All rights reserved.

Living Books is a registered trademark of Tyndale
House Publishers, Inc.

ISBN 0-8423-0488-6
Copyright © 1991 by Tyndale House Publishers, Inc.
All rights reserved
Printed in the United States of America

96 95 94 93 92
7 6 5 4 3 2

PUZZLES

ACROSS

1 "_____ a child to choose the right path, and when he is older, he will remain upon it" (Pro. 22:6)
4 Money institution workers (Isa. 24:2)
8 Hometown of Hebrew Temple attendants (Neh. 3:26)
9 Cloth makers (2 Ch. 2:7)
10 Animal group tenders (Gen. 13:7)
11 Carpenter; half brother of Jesus; N.T. author
13 Secret information gatherers (Gen. 42:8)
15 Maker of bread, cakes, and pastries (Gen. 40:1)
19 O.T. author who saw Jerusalem tested with a plumbline
20 Counselors (Act. 25:12)
23 Improve in value (Est. 2:13)
24 One to whom something belongs (Exo. 21:28)
25 Ones who shape and harden clay (Mat. 27:7)
26 "My strength evaporated like water on a _____ day" (Psa. 32:4)

DOWN

1 Prize gained by a victory (1 Th. 2:20)
2 Loathe; reject (Psa. 5:6)
3 Ship steerers (Eze. 27:8)
4 Archers (Jer. 51:3)
5 First boat builder (Gen. 6:13, 14)
6 Carry out a function or task (Exo. 12:12)
7 Regular order; set of procedures (2 Ch. 34:9)
12 Custodians (Est. 1:5)
14 Spokesman for God; foreteller of future (Deu. 13:1)
16 Fabricated; fictitious: 2 wds. (Jer. 23:32)
17 Deadly snakes of Middle East (Isa. 11:8)
18 "A curse on those who lead _____ the godly. But men who encourage the upright to do good shall be given a worthwhile reward" (Pro. 28:10)
21 Owner of threshing-floor that became Temple site (2 Ch. 3:1)
22 "At the name of Jesus every _____ shall bow in heaven and on earth and under the earth" (Phi. 2:10)

PUZZLE 1

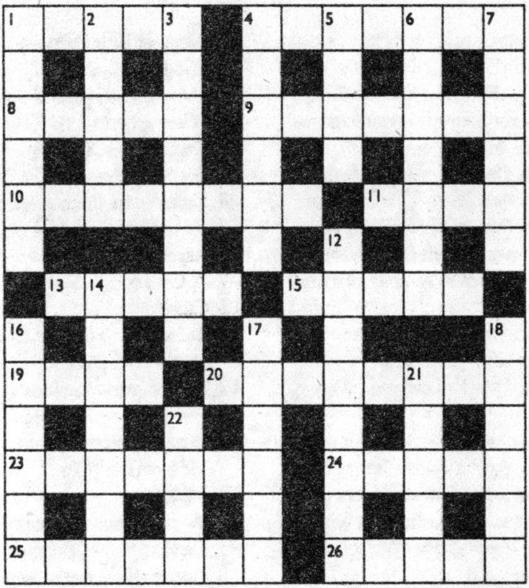

ACROSS

1 Separate grain from chaff (Jer. 51:2)
5 N.T. author who said, "Faith is dead if it is not the kind that results in good deeds"
9 Fixed the eyes in a steady, intent look (Act. 7:55)
10 Fisherman with two sons who became disciples (Mat. 4:21)
11 Managers of large sheep farms (2 Ki. 3:4)
13 Plow's circular steel part with sharp edge (1 Sa. 13:21)
15 Main activity of evil men (Pro. 2:11-14)
16 Take a long walk (Gen. 13:17)
20 Lie in wait to attack (Psa. 10:8)
21 Those who deal in objects of precious metal often set with gems (Exo. 35:35)
24 Discipline (Hab. 1:12)
25 Son of Aaron judged for using unholy fire (Lev. 10:1)
26 Indulged to excess (Jer. 50:10)
27 Assistant authority; one acting on behalf of another (1 Ki. 22:47)

DOWN

2 Judge of Israel between Jephthah and Elon (Jdg. 12:7-11)
3 Where Cain settled, east of Eden (Gen. 4:16)
4 Sorcerer; skillful person (Dan. 2:27)
5 Tasks to be done (Exo. 5:4)
6 Woman who aids at childbirth (Gen. 35:17)
7 Artist's rough drawing (2 Ki. 16:10)
8 Belonging to author of Proverbs chapter 30 (Pro. 30:1)
12 Pursue game for food (Gen. 27:5)
14 Employ for pay (Lev. 25:50)
15 Occupation of Hagar and Gehazi, for example (Gen. 16:1, 2; 2 Ki. 5:20)
17 What shepherds work with (Gen. 29:8)
18 Controlled a horse with bridle lines (2 Ki. 9:23)
19 Officially distribute (2 Ch. 31:19)
22 Royal decree or proclamation (Est. 3:14)
23 Unspecific very small amount: 2 wds.
25 Nearly correct or exact: abbr.

ACROSS

1 Excavated again, such as a well (Gen. 26:18)
4 Large bird in coastal areas (Lev. 11:16)
8 A hard gem (Exo. 28:17)
9 Tempted by arousing desire (Nah. 3:4)
10 Deerlike mammal related to the ox (Deu. 14:5)
11 Hebrew tribe appointed to offer animal sacrifices (1 Sa. 2:28)
13 Remains from burnt offerings (Lev. 4:12)
15 "The boy became so hungry that even the pods he was feeding the ____ looked good to him" (Luk. 15:16)
19 Jacob's funeral site in Canaan; threshing place (Gen. 50:10)
20 Young steers used as sacrifices (Psa. 50:9)
23 O.T. prophet who spoke against offering God sick animals; O.T. book
24 Brother who was angry when the Prodigal Son returned home (Luk. 15:28)
25 Settle snugly into a sheltered location (Isa. 34:15)
26 Scattered (Lev. 19:9)

DOWN

1 Ceremonial form or traditional procedure (Hos. 8:13)
2 Storage and distribution site (Jer. 38:11)
3 Slender, swift-running mammals of Africa and Asia (1 Ki. 4:23)
4 "Your teeth are white as ____ wool, newly shorn and washed" (Sg. 4:2)
5 Industrious insects working in colonies (Pro. 6:6)
6 Not pure; unapproved for Hebrew consumption (Lev. 7:19)
7 Endearing term for young boy (Luk. 7:14)
12 Small, migratory birds associated with sparrows (Psa. 84:3)
14 Horse barns (1 Ki. 4:28)
16 Large game fish of northern waters (Mat. 1:4)
17 Short-winged, stout-bodied game birds given to Hebrews in wilderness (Exo. 16:13)
18 Large hawk (Deu. 14:13)
21 Evergreen tree with aromatic, reddish wood used in Hebrew ceremonies (Lev. 14:49)
22 Recipient of proverbial messages from Agur (Pro. 30:1)

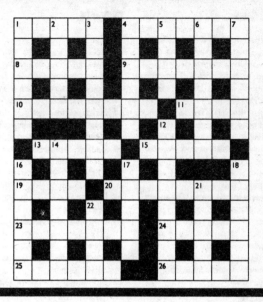

ACROSS

1 "There is a friend who sticks ____ than a brother" (Pro. 18:24)
5 "I took two shepherd's ____, naming one Grace and the other Union, and I fed the flock" (Zec. 11:7)
8 Me, reflexively (Gen. 16:5)
9 Elevated structures on which sheep are sacrificed (Exo. 20:24)
10 Curved upper support over an opening (Act. 4:11)
11 Contagious disease that spreads rapidly (1 Ki. 8:37)
13 Quote from Psalm 100:3 about our relationship to God: 4 wds.
16 Annual Hebrew ceremony when roast lamb is eaten with bitter herbs (Exo. 12:8, 11)
18 Salt Lake City's state
20 Flow of water from underground (Gen. 26:19)
22 "He leadeth me beside the still ____" (Psa. 23:2; KJV)
23 To David: "I chose you to be the ____ of my people Israel when you were tending your sheep in the pastureland" (2 Sa. 7:8)
24 Songs sung by abrupt alternations between a natural voice and a falsetto

DOWN

2 "On top of these blankets is placed a ____ of rams' skins, dyed red" (Exo. 26:14)
3 Sheep tenders (Gen. 46:32)
4 Rouse; stimulate; make like new again (Isa. 32:2)
5 Hindu religious teacher; yogi
6 Small, unusually wise insect (Pro. 30:24, 25)
7 Capable of producing abundant plant life (Gen. 13:10)
12 Completely tired or worn out (Gen. 25:29)
14 "Follow God's ____ in everything you do just as a much loved child imitates his father" (Eph. 5:1)
15 Thin; gaunt (Eze. 34:20)
17 Energy; force; determination (Psa. 38:19)
19 Month of the Hebrews' Exodus from Egypt (Deu. 16:1)
21 Ohio's neighbor: abbr.

PUZZLE 4

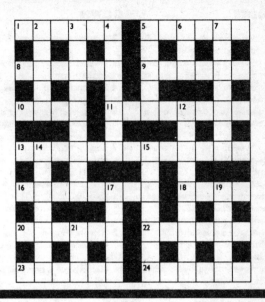

ACROSS

1 Boxlike containers (2 Ch. 34:17)
5 Building location (1 Ki. 6:7)
9 Quartz with various colors (Isa. 54:12)
10 External window covers or shades (Eze. 27:7)
11 Frameworks of crossed wood or metal strips (1 Ki. 7:21)
13 City given to tribe of Manasseh (1 Ch. 6:70)
15 Hand-held implement (Exo. 20:25)
16 Table supports (Exo. 25:26)
20 Unusually fine; valuable (Luk. 7:46)
21 Roof or ceiling window, such as in Noah's ark (Gen. 6:16)
24 Hardened wall coating (Dan. 5:5)
25 Where God gave Moses blueprints for building the Tabernacle (Heb. 12:18)
26 Short, weak sound, such as from a bird (Isa. 10:14)
27 Impress as important; give emphasis (Lev. 6:17)

DOWN

2 Central or essential part (Gen. 10:10)
3 Bring legal action; petition (Eze. 7:25)
4 Long, thin slats of wood (Num. 21:18)
5 "Those who hear my instructions and ignore them are foolish, like a man who builds his house on ____" (Mat. 7:26)
6 Occupants of a rented dwelling (Lev. 25:23)
7 Pointed metal fasteners for wood (Exo. 38:20)
8 Lending money at excessive interest (Amo. 5:11)
12 "Do not bring an ____ into your home and worship it" (Deu. 7:26)
14 Eternal home of the wicked (2 Th. 1:9)
15 Balcony or patio (Eze. 41:9)
17 Permanent underground home (2 Ki. 21:26)
18 Garment that hangs below the waist (Exo. 20:26)
19 "It is better to live in the corner of an ____ than with a crabby woman in a lovely home" (Pro. 21:9)
22 Groups of people, often assembled for crime (Hos. 6:9)
23 Place for the foot to go up or down (1 Ki. 10:20)
25 Respectful direct address to a man (Gen. 24:18)

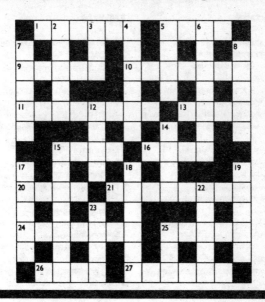

ACROSS

1 Requests (Gen. 46:33)
5 Shortened form
9 Long period of time
12 Blue: Ger.
13 Single stinging insect: 2 wds.
14 Make leather (Act. 9:43)
15 Condemn to eternal punishment
16 Most powerful one (Gen. 17:1)
18 Dwell
20 Related to ground: pref.
21 Imitated in mockery: slang
24 Ruth's mother-in-law (Rut. 1:15)
27 Deluded (Job 15:31)
31 Twist fibers into thread (Exo. 35:26)
32 What Peter sliced off (Joh. 18:10)
33 Microscopic hairs
35 Participle ending
36 Employed (Gen. 47:24)
38 Communication system (Gen. 10:5)
40 Celestial bodies (Gen. 1:16)
42 Knitting material (Eze. 27:19)
43 Obtain; select (Gen. 7:2)
45 Swine sounds
49 Initial (Exo. 22:15)
53 Witticism
54 Pidgeon talk
55 Pedestal part
56 Elbow-wrist connector
57 The ____ Commandments
58 Polluted fog
59 Wapitis

DOWN

1 Adoniram's father (1 Ki. 4:6)
2 Broad, flat piece
3 ____kaze
4 Topped ice cream
5 Motorists' aid organization: abbr.
6 Round, wooden cask: abbr. (2 Sa. 16:1)
7 Victor's award site: Gk. (Rom. 14:8)
8 Dominion (Gen. 10:11)
9 North African country (2 Ki. 19:9)
10 Long-tailed rodent (Lev. 11:29)
11 One, no matter which (Gen. 2:16)
17 Mardi ____
19 Long narrative poem
22 Began in the garden (Gen. 3:5)
23 Tarry (Num. 22:37)
25 Chinese dynasty
26 Present action suffix: med.
27 ____ ex machina
28 Earth's orbit direction (Gen. 2:8)
29 The world and all its parts (Rom. 8:19)
30 Mighty: pref.
34 Belonging to the fields: pref.
37 Forcefully pull (Exo. 21:14)
39 One-of-a-kind (1 Ch. 17:21)
41 Slide
44 Judean city (Jos. 15:34)
46 Invalid
47 Tight twist
48 Mineral spring resorts
49 Tenth month: abbr. (1 Ki. 8:2)
50 Fish eggs
51 Fuss
52 Felled tree (2 Ch. 2:16)

ACROSS

1 "Melchizedek had no father or mother and there is no ____ of any of his ancestors" (Heb. 7:3)
5 Interfere; fool with (2 Ch. 25:19)
8 First person to be deceived (2 Co. 11:3)
9 "Their ____ in the truth that they have been taught must be strong" (Tit. 1:9)
10 Widespread honor (2 Sa. 23:22)
11 Ornamental case for small articles used daily
12 "The Lord is the great Prosecuting ____ presenting his case against his people" (Isa. 3:13)
13 Outlawed; prohibited (1 Sa. 28:3)
15 Annoy with hostile intent (Ezr. 6:7)
17 Unintentional or chance mishap (Num. 35:22)
20 Catch one's breath with amazement (Jer. 49:17)
22 Sum of one's possessions (Luk. 12:13)
23 "He who ____ grace and truth is the king's friend" (Pro. 22:11)
24 Conservative Protestant organization of churches: abbr.
25 State firmly and positively (Est. 1:22)
26 Secretly watching to gather information (1 Sa. 28:9)

DOWN

2 Choose by vote (Num. 14:4)
3 "In my ____, nothing is worthwhile; everything is futile" (Ecc. 1:2)
4 Steal by trickery or deception (Lev. 19:11)
5 Rights and wrongs of a legal case (Dan. 9:18)
6 One who gives (Lev. 27:10)
7 "The king was furious but first consulted his ____, for he did nothing without their advice" (Est. 1:12, 13)
14 Charges with an offense (1 Cor. 6:6)
15 "A man's conscience is the Lord's searchlight exposing his hidden ____" (Pro. 20:27)
16 Lawfully; rightly (Gen. 31:16)
18 Visual representation of a likeness (Joh. 3:14)
19 "It would be an annual ____ from generation to generation" (Est. 9:28)
21 "In their foolishness they worshiped heathen idols despite the Lord's ____ warnings" (2 Ki. 17:15)

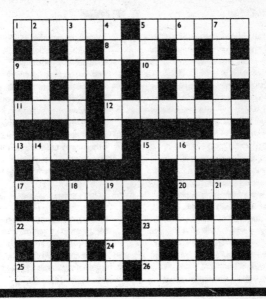

ACROSS

1 Ceremonial procession (1 Co. 4:9)
5 Strong winds and heavy rain, hail, or snow (Isa. 30:30)
8 Not private; visible and accessible to the community at large (Isa. 4:5)
9 "Never ____ yourselves. Leave that to God, for he has said that he will repay those who deserve it" (Rom. 12:19)
10 Olympic awards site: Gk.
11 Praises publicly, often by hand clapping (Psa. 49:18)
13 Quote from Jesus about his return to earth: 4 wds. (Rev. 22:6)
16 "One shall come who rules righteously.... He shall be ... as ____ after rain" (2 Sa. 23:3, 4)
18 Food served and eaten at one sitting (Gen. 18:16)
20 Standards of excellence; worthy goals (Psa. 26:3)
22 Malta and Patmos, for example (Rev. 1:9)
23 Ruler; son of God, the King (Act. 5:31)
24 Flying, biting insect that annoys livestock (Jer. 46:20)

DOWN

2 Mistreatment (Mat. 27:39)
3 "Kingdoms will try to strengthen themselves by forming ____ with each other (Dan. 2:43)
4 "Fill the followers of God with joy. Let those who love your salvation ____, 'What a wonderful God he is'" (Psa. 70:4)
5 Pound upon with one's feet or other heavy objects (Gen. 49:19)
6 "I ____ no one anything. Everything under the heaven is mine" (Job 41:11)
7 "They gathered all the armies of the world near a place called, in Hebrew, Armageddon—the Mountain of ____" (Rev. 16:16)
12 Gathered together (Act. 10:27)
14 "What therefore God hath joined together, let not man put ____" (Mk. 10:9; KJV)
15 Requiring (2 Co. 1:4)
17 Point of controversy (Jdg. 11:26)
19 Jesus "died to ____ that whole system of Jewish laws"; make legally void (Eph. 2:15)
21 Eastern border town of the Hebrews' Promised Land (Num. 34:10, 11)

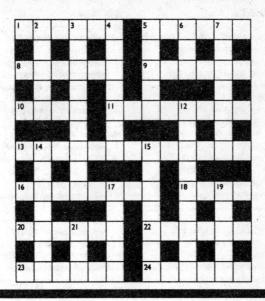

ACROSS

1 Great Hebrew lawgiver (Joh. 1:17)
4 Paupers; solicitors of charity (Luk. 14:21)
8 Public announcer (Isa. 40:9)
9 Senior commissioned military officer (Jdg. 4:7)
10 Trained participants in competitive sports (2 Ki. 2:16)
11 Spouse (Jer. 5:8)
13 Person doing business on behalf of another (Luk. 10:22)
15 "These teachers in their ____ will tell you anything to get hold of your money" (2 Pe. 2:3)
19 Coarse, woven fabrics to sleep on (Mk. 6:55)
20 Twelve disciples (Luk. 9:1)
23 Protected by a defensive covering (Eze. 38:4)
24 A Pharaoh of Egypt in Jeremiah's prophecy (Jer. 46:2)
25 One in charge of daily operations for a business or household (Gen. 43:16)
26 Cook by dry heat (Ex. 12:8)

DOWN

1 Saul's daughter; David's wife (2 Sa. 3:13)
2 "I have created the ____ who blows the coals beneath the forge and makes the weapons of destruction" (Isa. 54:16)
3 Noncommissioned military officer (Mat. 27:54)
4 Military trumpeter (1 Co. 14:8)
5 "Young men who are wise obey the law; a son who is a member of a lawless ____ is a shame to his father" (Pro. 28:7)
6 Land area measurement (Eze. 36:34)
7 "In every contract of sale there must be a stipulation that the land can be redeemed at any time by the ____" (Lev. 25:24)
12 Person incarcerated or on trial (Act. 25:14)
14 Keepers of Hebrew Temple entrances (Eze. 44:11)
16 What morticians do to a corpse (Gen. 50:2)
17 "Every house built by the wicked is as fragile as a ____ web" (Job. 27:18)
18 One who accompanies another (Gen. 12:20)
21 Roman province on southern coast of Asia Minor (Act. 27:5)
22 "Don't ____ about your plans for tomorrow—wait and see what happens" (Pro. 27:1)

ACROSS

1 "Stay away from where the prostitute walks, lest she ____ you and seduce you" (Pro. 7:25)
4 Itinerant Levitical teacher (2 Ch. 17:8)
8 Dishonest or mischievous person; scoundrel
9 Distress arising from a sense of guilt (Psa. 51:17)
10 Charging another with wrongdoing (Luk. 23:14)
11 Dull, persistent pain; yearning (2 Co. 6:10)
13 Used profane language (Exo. 5:21)
15 "If you call your friend an ____ [foolish person], you are in danger of being brought before the court" (Mat. 5:22)
19 Skills; branches of learning, such as the occult (Exo. 7:22)
20 Sexual unfaithfulness of a married person (Exo. 20:14)
23 Feeling humiliated, disgraced, or guilty (2 Sa. 19:5)
24 Person outstanding in size, power, or achievement
25 Expected deliverer of the Jews (Psa. 110:1)
26 Periods of about 365 days (Gen. 5:3)

DOWN

1 Expression of intention to harm (2 Sa. 12:10)
2 "No Israeli may practice black ____, or call on the evil spirits for aid, or be a fortune-teller" (Deu. 18:10)
3 "Wherever your ____ is, there your heart and thoughts will also be" (Luk. 12:34)
4 Harsh ruler having absolute power (Rev. 11:7)
5 Idle, worthless vagabonds (Isa. 5:11)
6 Canaanite city where Achan angered God by stealing loot (Jos. 6:26–7:1)
7 "He heard the warning and wouldn't listen; the fault is his. If he had ____ the warning, he would have saved his life" (Eze. 33:5)
12 Worshiping images of a god (Num. 31:1)
14 Women believed to have occult powers (Isa. 8:19)
16 Prophet hired by Moab to curse the Hebrews (Num. 22:7)
17 Southern Judean city near Edom (Jos. 15:21, 22)
18 Carnivorous African and Asian mammals with powerful jaws (Isa. 13:22)
21 Additional (Lev. 21:18)
22 Ahab's father; one of Israel's most wicked kings (1 Ki. 16:25, 28)

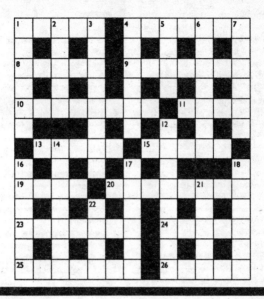

ACROSS

1 Sweet, yellow-rinded melon
7 Where Jacob wrestled with the Angel (Gen. 32:30)
13 Sacred choral composition (Isa. 27:2)
14 Treat as equals
15 Difficult to control (Gen. 49:4)
16 "____ wrong way": 2 wds.; cause irritation
17 Cathedral
18 More just and equitable than another (Lev. 19:15)
19 "Father who is over us ____ in us": 2 wds. (Eph. 4:6)
21 Woman's name
22 Characterized by great effort and care (Ezr. 6:12)
24 Current enlistment date: mil. abbr.
25 Placed; positioned (Gen. 1:17)
26 Cathode ray tube: computer abbr.
29 Tenth book of the N.T.
35 Father of Azareel (Neh. 11:13; KJV)
37 Trademark for polyester fiber
38 Repeated statements of falsehood (1 Ki. 22:23)
39 Chins
40 Run a stake through a body: var.
41 Class of criminal gangs in India
42 Scorcher (Isa. 49:10)
43 Tree trunk extension (Eze. 15:2)
44 Betty ____
45 Intervals of passing time

DOWN

1 Toward the posterior end
2 Annual rings of trees
3 Walk leisurely (2 Sa. 11:2)
4 One of the two Zorathite clans (1 Ch. 4:2)
5 Be the property of (Gen. 32:18)
6 Friend: law
7 Completed; matured (Joh. 17:23)
8 Moses "performed miracles that have never been ____d" (Deu. 34:11)
9 Ancient kingdom along the southern Nile River
10 Relating to medical treatment: suff.
11 Colorless, flammable, gaseous hydrocarbon
12 Looked at another maliciously
20 Those who regard with contempt or disdain (Act. 13:41)
23 O.T. book between Ezra and Esther: abbr.
26 Philippine two-wheeled carriage
27 Poet
28 A great merchant in China
29 Large birds
30 Winged fruit of ash or elm tree
31 Extensive frozen perennial cover
32 Pertaining to Moab's northern border river (Num. 21:13)
33 Observe (Num. 15:39)
34 Scythe handles
36 Something entangling the unwary (Eze. 17:20)
41 Twice as much: abbr. (Deu. 21:17)

ACROSS

1 Country just north of Israel (Jdg. 1:26)
4 Inhabitants of major Mediterranean island (Act. 2:11)
8 King of Egypt during battle of Carchemish (Jer. 46:2)
9 Giant race in ancient Transjordan (Deu. 3:11)
10 Descendants of Abraham through Ishmael (Neh. 4:7)
11 Circle of light around a body (Eze. 1:27)
13 "Issue a royal edict, a law of the ____ and Persians that can never be changed" (Est. 1:19)
15 "The heart of Nimrod's empire included Babel, ____, Accad, and Calneh in the land of Shinar" (Gen. 10:10)
19 Scent as perceived by one's sense of smell (Num. 28:6)
20 Abraham's ancestral race (Deu. 26:5)
23 Ancient Roman region in Golan Heights; Texas city (Luk. 3:1)
24 Put to death by mob action (Jer. 12:6)
25 "'Show me a coin. Whose portrait is this on it?' They replied, '____—the Roman emperor's'" (Luk. 20:24)
26 Another name for Mount Hermon (Deu. 3:9)

DOWN

1 Day of Jesus' resurrection (Joh. 20:1)
2 Ruled: Lat.; Last part of the intestine: pl.
3 Original Canaanite tribe in north Transjordan defeated by Moses (Deu. 1:4)
4 Home of Simon, who carried Jesus' cross (Mat. 27:32)
5 Broad public display of goods or services: abbr.
6 Language of ancient Babylon (Dan. 2:4)
7 Hebrew champion captured and blinded by the Philistines (Jdg. 16:23)
12 Prickly shrubs; meaning of threshing place of Atad (Gen. 50:10)
14 Descendant of Esau living south of the Dead Sea (Gen. 36:9)
16 Type of law given by God at Mount Sinai (Joh. 7:22)
17 "We are no longer Jews or ____, but we are all the same—we are Christians; we are one in Christ Jesus" (Gal. 3:28)
18 Jewish queen of Persia
21 Moab's northern border river (Num. 21:13)
22 One of Ishmael's 12 sons; ancestor of tribe bearing his name (Gen. 25:12-16)

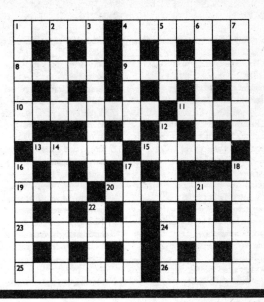

ACROSS

1. "Suddenly, the angel was joined by a vast host of others—the ____ of heaven—praising God" (Luk. 2:13)
5. Devices for holding things together (Exo. 26:6)
8. ____ and aah
9. "The Lord God said to the serpent, 'You shall ____ in the dust as long as you live'" (Gen. 3:14)
10. Pierce with a pointed pole (Gen. 40:19)
11. Ran away (Gen. 14:10)
12. Foot soldiers (2 Sa. 8:4)
14. Intense fear and panic (Gen. 42:21)
17. Plant bearing pods
19. Humility; shame; dishonor (Eze. 32:30)
21. Objects used to make a decision by chance (1 Ch. 6:61)
23. Chronological records of a king's wars and history (1 Ki. 14:19)
25. Association for a common purpose (Jer. 41:2)
26. Highest possible: abbr. (Eze. 27:10)
27. Flee (Gen. 19:17)
28. Hebrew name for God

DOWN

2. Nonurban; related to the country (Neh. 10:37)
3. One who enters for conquest (Jer. 50:44)
4. Person in military service (1 Sa. 18:17)
5. Highest in rank (Gen. 37:36)
6. Poisonous African snake
7. "I am but a ____ here on earth: how I need a map—and your commands are my chart and guide" (Psa. 119:19)
13. "A dull ____ requires great strength; be wise and sharpen the blade" (Ecc. 10:10)
15. "King Uzziah produced ____ of war manufactured in Jerusalem, invented by brilliant men to shoot arrows and huge stones" (2 Ch. 26:15)
16. Unit of electrical resistance
17. "Neither you nor anyone else can serve two masters. You will hate one and show ____ to the other" or vice versa (Luk. 16:13)
18. Philistine giant David defeated (1 Sa. 17:48, 49)
20. "Without making a big ____ over it, God simply shatters the greatest of men and puts others in their places" (Job 34:24)
22. Agreement to not fight (Deu. 20:10)
24. Solomon's great-grandson, a mostly-good king of Judah (Mat. 1:7)

26

ACROSS

1 "The Lord accepted Job's prayer on their ____"; interest or benefit (Job 42:9)
5 Plain or wasteland of the Jordan River valley (Deu. 3:17)
8 "Don't ____ the poor and sick! For the Lord is their defender"; steal from (Pro. 22:22)
9 Outdoor sports arenas
10 O.T. book predicting Jesus' virgin birth
11 "You made all the delicate, inner parts of my body and ____ them together in my mother's womb"; interlaced (Psa. 139:13)
12 Schooled; trained (1 Ch. 27:32)
14 Fulfilling; bringing about (Gen. 11:6)
17 "What a foundation you stand on now: the ____ and the prophets; and the cornerstone of the building is Jesus Christ himself"; disciples (Eph. 2:20)
19 "What fools the nations are to ____ against the Lord! How strange that men should try to outwit God"; be violently angry (Psa. 2:1)
21 On fire
23 "I was not called to be a missionary by any group or ____. My call is from Jesus Christ himself"; administrative department (Gal. 1:1)
24 One's relatives (Gen. 16:12)
25 Starts (1 Co. 14:36)
26 Indelibly mark human skin (Lev. 19:28)

DOWN

2 "What dainty morsels rumors are. They are ____ with great relish"; consumed (Pro. 18:8)
3 Supplements (2 Co. 7:13)
4 Making another appear guilty (Mk. 15:10)
5 Son of Aaron killed for using unholy fire (Num. 3:2, 4)
6 Expression of triumph (Psa. 35:25)
7 Rebekah's race (Gen. 25:20)
13 "A woman must not wear men's clothing, and a man must not wear women's clothing. This is ____ to the Lord your God"; detestable (Deu. 22:5)
15 "Find some ____, godly, honest men who hate bribes, and appoint them as judges"; competent (Exo. 18:21)
16 Moment (Luk. 1:44)
18 Onion-like herbs (Num. 11:5)
20 Small, insect-eating lizard (Lev. 11:30)
22 Descendant of King Solomon's officials who came to Jerusalem with Zerubbabel (Ezr. 2:55, 57)

28

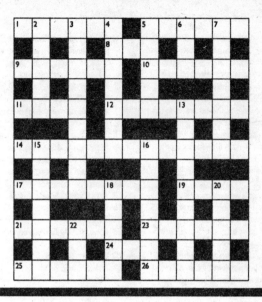

ACROSS

1 Moses' father-in-law (Exo. 3:1)
5 "____ fear and doubt! For remember, the Lord your God is with you wherever you go"; expel (Jos. 1:9)
8 "What's the ____ of saying that you have faith and are Christians if you aren't proving it by helping others?"; sense (Jam. 2:14)
9 Struck with amazement or horror (Dan. 4:19)
10 "Solomon was the ____ of 3,000 proverbs and wrote 1,005 songs"; originator (1 Ki. 4:32)
11 Flesh of a steer or cow (Isa. 25:6)
12 "Don't associate with ____"; persons advocating extreme change (Pro. 24:21)
14 Music played as support or embellishment (1 Ch. 25:1)
17 Refrains from (Act. 15:29)
19 Slippery liquids for fuel or lubrication (2 Ki. 20:13)
21 "I give them eternal life and they shall never perish. No one shall ____ them away from me"; suddenly grab away (Joh. 10:28)
23 "Caiaphas, who was High Priest that year, said, 'You stupid ____ let this one man die for the people'"; foolish persons (Joh. 11:49)
24 Judean village given to Caleb (Jos. 21:12, 16)
25 Conscious but not sensible, as in a drunken ____ (Gen. 9:24)
26 "Foolish and unlearned questions avoid, knowing that they do ____ strifes"; cause (2 Ti. 2:23; KJV)

DOWN

2 "They that wait upon the Lord shall renew their strength. They shall mount up with wings like ____": sing. (Isa. 40:31)
3 Frozen dew (Exo. 16:14; KJV)
4 Part of a rock stratum that appears above the ground (Sg. 2:14)
5 Facial hair on a man (Lev. 14:9)
6 Hard-shelled fruit with edible kernels (Gen. 43:11)
7 Enlarged from within (Deu. 8:4)
13 Disturbance; ruckus (Mk. 5:39)
15 A body of advisers (Est. 1:5)
16 Building an egg shelter (Num. 24:21)
18 One of King David's sons (1 Ch. 3:6)
20 Despise (Eze. 36:31; KJV)
22 Pointed end of something (Luk. 16:24)

ACROSS

1 Restaurant
5 Smallest particle
9 Engaged services of (2 Sa. 10:6)
10 Major Philistine city (Gen. 26:1)
12 Treat with scorn (Lam. 2:16)
13 Careened (Psa. 18:7)
15 Fool: Gk.
16 Notice of intent: abbr.
18 Hitler's party
19 Sick (Luk. 9:11)
20 Tabernacle choir leader (1 Ch. 16:7)
22 Achieve victory (Gen. 32:25)
23 False; fake: pref.
25 Hole (Eze. 8:7)
27 Same: Br.
29 Auto club: abbr.
30 Dilute solution of acetic acid (Psa. 69:21)
34 Stretch (Exo. 4:6)
38 Single unit (Gen. 2:24)
39 Decree (Exo. 20:1)
41 Female deer
42 Yellow Dutch cheese balls
44 Basketball organization: abbr.
45 Radical religious group (Act. 6:9)
46 Long, angry speech
48 Another name for Kiriath-jearim (Jos. 15:9)
50 Bottomless pit
51 Encourages; incites
52 Sweet potatoes
53 Glass part of camera

DOWN

1 Sphere (Psa. 25:13)
2 Operetic vocal solo
3 Provided food (Exo. 16:32)
4 "The land lies fair as ____ Garden in all its beauty" (Joe. 2:3)
5 King hearing Paul's defense (Act. 26:1)
6 Letter before U
7 Son of Jerahmeel (1 Ch. 2:25)
8 Lake in African Rift Valley
9 "I am the Lord who ____ you" (Exo. 15:26)
11 Syrian king (2 Ki. 15:37)
12 Fall in drops (Joe. 3:18)
14 Minor surface damage
17 One-and-only: abbr.
20 Short proverb
21 "Love the Lord your God with all your ____" (Mat. 22:37)
24 Employ for a purpose (Gen. 9:2)
26 National Association of Evangelicals: abbr.
28 Lack of restraint or reason (Ecc. 10:12)
30 ____ ganger; immature African locust
31 Eastern extent of Media-Persia (Est. 1:1)
32 Not far away (Gen. 41:48)
33 A cut of meat (Num. 6:20)
35 Grown-ups (Luk. 1:17)
36 Carbonated soft drinks
37 Son of Canaan (Gen. 10:15)
40 Group of secret conspirators
43 Language of Indians in southern Mexico
45 Recent or novel: pref.
47 District sales manager: abbr.
49 Honest ____ (Illinois politician)

PUZZLE 16

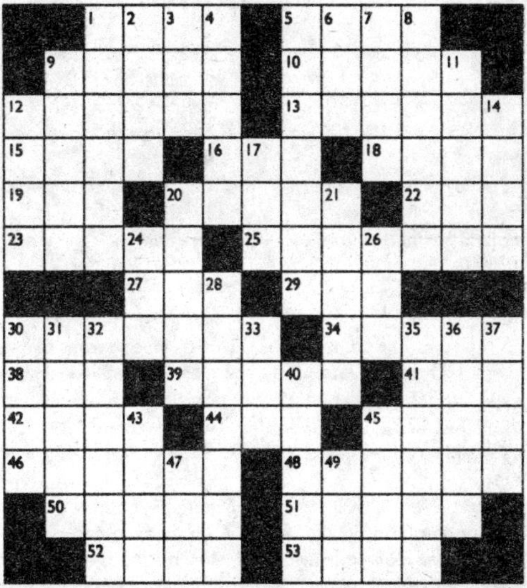
1
2
3
4
5
6
7
8
9
10
11
12
13
14
15
16
17
18
19
20
21
22
23
24
25
26
27
28
29
30
31
32
33
34
35
36
37
38
39
40
41
42
43
44
45
46
47
48
49
50
51
52
53

ACROSS

1 Song of praise or gladness (Isa. 27:2)
5 Hymn ending (Psa. 41:13)
9 Choir members' dress (1 Ch. 15:27)
10 "Always be full of joy in the Lord; I say it again, ____" (Phi. 4:4)
11 Pleasing arrangements of musical notes (Psa. 33:2)
13 Stimulate; heighten, such as a sense (Deu. 32:41)
15 "Sing his praises, accompanied by music from the harp and lute and ____"; ancient stringed instrument (Psa. 92:3)
16 Naomi's wealthy relative in Judah (Rut. 2:1)
20 Direct a choir (Neh. 12:46)
21 Small tambourines (Psa. 68:25)
24 High-pitched tune made through the lips and teeth (Zec. 10:8)
25 "The first musician—the inventor of the harp and flute" (Gen. 4:21)
26 Author of last part of Book of Proverbs (Pro. 30:1)
27 Making an effort; attempting (Gen. 44:15)

DOWN

2 Abigail's first husband, a sheepherder (1 Sa. 25:3, 4)
3 Belonging to a man
4 Feel surprise and wonder (Psa. 48:5)
5 City in tribe of Benjamin (Neh. 11:31)
6 Friend of Job's who came to comfort him (Job 2:11)
7 Skin-covered percussion instruments (Psa. 81:2)
8 Rhythmic stresses in music
12 Plain where Nebuchadnezzar's band signaled worship of his 90-foot statue (Dan. 3:1, 5)
14 Toothed, hair arrangement tool (Job 33:10)
15 Jumping, often with joy (Mal. 4:2)
17 "In the twinkling of an eye, when the last trumpet is ____, all the Christians who have died will suddenly become alive" (1 Co. 15:52)
18 "In everything you do, put God first, and he will ____ you and crown your efforts with success" (Pro. 3:6)
19 Sacred song giving its name to an O.T. book (Act. 13:33)
22 Son of Gad; grandson of Jacob (Gen. 46:16)
23 "I, Jesus, am the bright Morning ____" (Rev. 22:16)
25 "So be truly glad! There is wonderful ____ ahead, even though the going is rough for a while down here" (1 Pe. 1:6)

PUZZLE 17

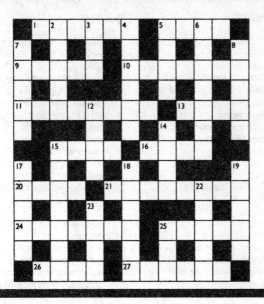

ACROSS

1 O.T. prophet and author: abbr.
5 Long, rigid, round item (Exo. 26:28)
8 Floating platform (1 Ki. 5:9)
12 Religious teacher at Water Gate (Neh. 8:1)
13 Mist; haze: Scot.
14 Son of Shelah (Luk. 3:35)
15 Family head in tribe of Gad (Num. 26:15, 18)
16 Reserve officer candidate: abbr.
17 Changed: pref.
18 Span of one's existence (Gen. 4:26)
20 Country Chedorlaomer ruled (Gen. 14:1)
21 Proceeded toward (Gen. 31:21)
23 Return to proper condition (Num. 4:32)
27 Refugee from a revolution
31 Growing older (1 Sa. 17:12)
32 Suitors
33 German author
35 Element used in antiseptics
36 Cyprus or Crete, e.g. (Jer. 2:11)
38 "So be it" (Deu. 27:15)
41 Meddlesome person (1 Pe. 4:15)
46 Person celebrated for accomplishments (2 Ki. 5:1)
47 Rock mined for its contents
48 Australian Boating Industry Association: abbr.
49 Southern Judean city (Jos. 15:20, 26)
50 Women's Army Corps: abbr.
51 Deficiency (Exo. 16:18)
52 Extremely skinny (Gen. 41:19)
53 Satellite-to-satellite tracking: abbr.
54 Concept (Amo. 5:18)

DOWN

1 Enthusiastic devotion (Psa. 69:9)
2 King David's estate manager (1 Ch. 27:26)
3 Highest-ranking teacher: abbr.
4 Unplowed strip in cultivated field
5 Mortician
6 Pleaasant odor (Gen. 27:17)
7 Draw back (Psa. 18:15)
8 Cured (Deu. 28:27)
9 First martyr (Mat. 23:35)
10 White goat cheese
11 Streetcar: Br.
19 Legs between hips and knees (Job 40:17)
22 Include as part of a unified whole
23 Musical style
24 Self-image
25 Filled, baked pastry shell
26 Equally true but seemingly contradictory truths
28 Guaranteed annual income: abbr.
29 Operate regularly (Gen. 39:5)
30 Compass point about 4:00
34 Arm joints (Mk. 7:3)
35 Small, multi-segmented creature (Psa. 105:31)
37 Invisible emanations
38 Judean king in Elijah's time (1 Ki. 17:1)
39 Short note (2 Sa. 11:6)
40 Ephraimite clan founder (Num. 26:34, 35)
42 Indonesian island near Java
43 O.T. prophet to Edom: abbr.
44 Numbered cubes (Jos. 14:2)
45 African Bantu people

PUZZLE 18

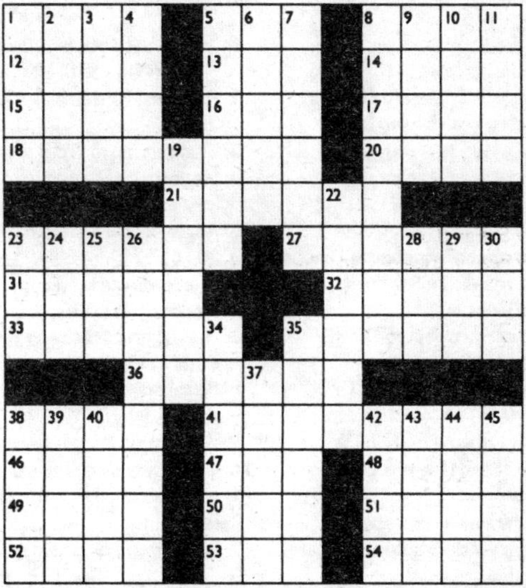

ACROSS

1 Jesus ____
7 Local church leaders (1 Pe. 5:1)
13 Expression of pleasure or triumph
14 Related to body's main blood vessel
15 "Quick! Mix ____ pancakes!": 2 wds. (Gen. 18:6)
16 Crawly
17 Huge mammal with horned snout
18 Publisher William Randolph ____
19 Grease: Scot.
21 Deserter from Saul to David (1 Ch. 12:20)
22 "Is anything too ____ for God?" (Gen. 18:14)
23 Son of Hotham (1 Ch. 7:35)
26 Female sheep (Num. 6:14)
27 Male cat
28 South Africa Airways: abbr.
31 Languages including Lao, Shan, etc.
32 Fish; rockling
36 Feather-like column of smoke
38 Pushed out by force (Exo. 10:11)
40 Refuse to notice (2 Ch. 6:42)
42 "Carve ____ on it, and that's his god" (Isa. 40:20)
43 Light-sensitive eyeball lining
44 Son of Javan (Gen. 10:4)
45 Flower with narrow, sword-shaped leaves
46 Restless; troubled
47 Bloodsucking African fly
48 Spas: Br.

DOWN

1 "Upon this rock I will build my ____" (Mat. 16:18)
2 Egyptian Pharaoh aiding Judah (Jer. 37:5)
3 Brighter; more promising
4 Smoothed and pressed by a hot implement
5 Aegean island visited by Paul (Act. 20:15)
6 "He leads me beside ____ quiet streams" (Psa. 23:2)
7 "Let us practice loving ____ other" (1 Jo. 4:7)
8 Pertaining to traditional knowledge
9 Anxious or fearful anitcipation
10 Of endless duration: arch.
11 Large-toothed tool to cut with the grain
12 Long, round-bladed mowing tool
20 "What ____ God wrought"
24 Memorandum of agreement: abbr.
25 In the middle of
28 Third Person of the Trinity (1 Pe. 1:2)
29 Horatio ____ : poss.
30 Father's or mother's sister: infor.
31 Steel sheets coated with lead and tin
32 Endowed with ability (Act. 15:32)
33 An exemplar; archetype
34 A determination: Lat.
35 Belonging to an estranged person (Exo. 23:4)
37 Damp (Eze. 31:4)
39 Drippy day? (Pro. 27:15)
41 Freedom from work and worry (Gen. 27:39)
44 Kushiro, Japan airport symbol

ACROSS

1 His body was bound on an altar by his father (Gen. 22:9)
5 To make an effusive display of sentiment (Psa. 104:10)
8 "There will come a time when your limbs will tremble with age, your strong legs will become weak, and your _____ will be too few to do their work" (Ecc. 12:3)
9 "Where is the _____ King of the Jews? for we have seen his star in far-off eastern lands and have come to worship him" (Mat. 2:2)
11 Desire for food (Job 33:20)
13 Masticate; grind in the mouth (Lev. 11:26)
15 "When a good man _____, he leaves an inheritance to his grandchildren" (Pro. 13:22)
16 "Don't eavesdrop! You may _____ your servant cursing you" (Ecc. 7:21)
20 Lacking hair on the head (Lev. 13:40)
21 Unintentional mishap (Num. 16:29)
24 "The devil who had betrayed them will again be thrown into the Lake of Fire burning with _____"; nonmetallic chemical element (Rev. 20:10)
25 Group of church singers (Rev. 14:2)
26 Jaw part (Lev. 13:29)
27 People between childhood and maturity (Isa. 40:30)

DOWN

2 "If you love _____, you will end in poverty. Stay awake, work hard, and there will be plenty to eat" (Pro. 20:13)
3 Cremation remains (Exo. 27:3)
4 Soundness of mind (Dan. 4:34)
5 Woman's loose, flowing outer garment (Pro. 31:22)
6 Kill by depriving of air (1 Ki. 3:19)
7 "A dry crust eaten in peace is better than _____ every day along with argument and strife"; thick slice of meat (Pro. 17:1)
10 Reports of recent events (Gen. 32:6)
12 One Philistine giant had six of these on each foot (2 Sa. 21:20)
14 Jesus' grandfather (Luk. 3:23)
15 Samson's girlfriend and betrayer (Jdg. 16:19)
17 Wanes, such as life; declines slowly (Lev. 26:16)
18 Vitamin-deficiency disease (Deu. 28:27)
19 Absolute, such as naked (Psa. 55:4)
22 First person who didn't die (Heb. 11:5)
23 Lean or slender (Job 33:21)
25 Hospital ward for heart patients: abbr.

PUZZLE 20

ACROSS

1 Is unwilling to acknowledge or accept (Eze. 14:7)
5 Series of visions during sleep (Joe. 2:28)
8 "Although the man and his wife were both _____, neither of them was embarrassed or ashamed" (Gen. 2:25)
9 Professional tree harvesters (2 Ch. 2:18)
10 "Tell them, '_____, the God of your ancestors Abraham, Isaac, and Jacob, has sent me to you.' This is my eternal name" (Exo. 3:15)
12 Judean king to whom God said, "Ask me for a sign. Ask anything you like, in heaven or on earth" (Isa. 7:11)
16 God's characteristic of being sympathetic, showing pity (Exo. 22:27)
18 "You will experience God's peace, which is far more wonderful than the human _____ can understand" (Phi. 4:7)
20 Declare ahead; foretell (Act. 11:28)
22 Even if you are stained as red as _____, I can make you white as wool"; deep red color (Isa. 1:18)
24 Surrender; cease resistance (Psa. 119:87)
25 Jericho woman who helped Hebrew spies (Jam. 2:25)
26 "Lord, be _____ above the highest heavens"; glorified (Psa. 57:5)

DOWN

1 Money paid for use of another's property (Sg. 8:11)
2 City of Judah in hill country (Jos. 15:56)
3 Food chewed again by ruminating animals (Lev. 11:2)
4 Confidence in one's own abilities: 2 wds. (Isa. 3:18)
5 Canine (Exo. 11:7)
6 City in heart of Nimrod's empire (Gen. 10:10)
7 Conventional title for married woman: abbr. from Fr.
11 A son of Joktan (Gen. 10:26, 28)
13 Midianite general who gave his name to a winepress (Jdg. 7:25)
14 Filthy film on a liquid (Psa. 119:119)
15 "The _____ of the Lord will last forever. And his message is the Good News that was preached to you" (1 Pe. 1:24, 25)
17 Belonging to times long past (Num. 13:22)
19 Horse's cry (Jer. 50:11)
21 Prophet of God in Samaria (2 Ch. 28:9)
22 People to whom seventh N.T. book was written: abbr.
23 Cry: wail (Gen. 27:34)
24 Affirmative salute given Jesus in jest by Roman soldiers (Mk. 15:18)

PUZZLE 21

ACROSS

1 American Association of Retired Persons: abbr.
5 Fixed charge (Exo. 22:15)
8 Boundary city for Asher (Jos. 19:25)
12 Burn evidence (Lev. 13:28)
13 Night-flying bird (Lev. 11:17)
14 ____hausen; W. Germany city
15 Black; dark
16 King: Sp.
17 Region in Ethiopia (Isa. 43:3)
18 Observing (1 Sa. 26:12)
20 Son of Naomi (Rut. 1:1)
22 Born as
23 Mimic: slang
24 Difficult situation (Gen. 30:22)
27 Walking sticks (Num. 21:18)
31 ____ Dodds (athlete)
32 Son of Bela (1 Ch. 7:7)
33 Cantaloupes, for one (Num. 11:5)
37 Colored, valuable quartz (Exo. 28:20)
40 Computer-aided instruction: abbr.
41 Father of Phinehas, a priest (1 Sa. 1:3)
42 Belonging to Othniel's uncle (Jos. 15:17)
45 Separate chaff from grain (Jer. 51:2)
49 Region (Gen. 13:13)
50 "____ for ____, tooth for tooth" (Lev. 24:20)
52 Recognition (1 Ch. 14:17)
53 Look over quickly
54 Belief system: abbr.
55 An institution of higher learning: abbr.
56 Belonging to Zophah's son (1 Ch. 7:36)
57 Donkey (Gen. 16:12)
58 After a certain time (Exo. 13:10)

DOWN

1 Tag on sale item: 2 wds.
2 Face disease
3 Smooth with tines
4 Snooping
5 Unable to recall (Deu. 6:13)
6 Female sheep (Num. 6:14)
7 Cyprian sorcerer (Act. 13:8)
8 King of Israel (2 Ki. 15:30)
9 Israeli city (2 Sa. 20:14)
10 ____ Hamath; Israeli border town (Num. 34:7)
11 Iraq's eastern neighbor
19 Rebuilder of Jerusalem's walls: abbr.
21 Suitable (Isa. 1:10)
24 Pacific Garden Mission: abbr.
25 Recline (Rut. 3:4)
26 Sick (1 Sa. 5:12)
28 Very important person: abbr.
29 Prior
30 Respectful address (Gen. 23:11)
34 Large bodies of salt water (Gen. 1:9)
35 Arrest: slang
36 Canaanite general (Jdg. 4:2)
37 Polished, precious stones (Gen. 24:53)
38 Muhammad ____ (boxer)
39 Wicked (Deu. 10:16)
42 Currency (1 Ki. 21:2)
43 Oil company name
44 Guide (Exo. 3:10)
46 Grandmother: infor.
47 Leave out (Lev. 5:16)
48 "____ a story to tell to the nations"
51 Affirmative statement (Gen. 3:12)

PUZZLE 22

ACROSS

1 Structures to offer sacrifices (Exo. 20:24)
5 Small magical symbols (Act. 19:19)
8 Father of Bezalel, the craftsman (Exo. 31:1)
9 "Everyone who asks, receives; all who seek, find; and the door is opened to everyone who ____"; raps (Luk. 11:10)
10 Basely (2 Sa. 1:21;KJV)
11 Opposed to (Isa. 60:14)
12 Formal confederation between nations (Dan. 11:17)
14 "Have faith and love, and enjoy the ____ of those who love the Lord and have pure hearts"; close association (2 Ti. 2:22)
17 "The stone rejected by the builders has now become the ____ of the arch"; top piece (Psa. 118:22)
19 "Reverence for God ____ hours to each day"; increases (Pro. 10:27)
21 Acts of bearing young (Exo. 28:10)
23 "As the ____ pot for silver, and the furnace for gold; so is a man to his praise"; purifying (Pro. 27:21;KJV)
24 Time before night
25 Deceivers and swindlers (1 Co. 5:10)
26 Moved quickly out of the way (1 Sa. 19:10)

DOWN

2 Cloth made from flax (Exo. 26:1)
3 "Say to ____, 'Be sure that you do all the Lord has told you to.'"; friend of Paul (Col. 4:17)
4 "A man's courage can ____ his broken body, but when courage dies, what hope is left?"; provide nourishment for (Pro. 18:14)
5 "Any kingdom filled with ____ war is doomed; so is a home filled with argument and strife"; domestic (Luk. 11:17)
6 "God is Light and in him is no darkness at ____"; so much (1 Jo. 1:5)
7 Last book of the O.T.
13 Refrained (Act. 15:29)
15 O.T. prophetic book to Edom
16 Served too much food (Deu. 32:15)
18 Fertile areas in a desert (Hos. 13:15)
20 Leap or skip about (1 Ki. 18:26)
22 "They are asking a piece of wood to tell them what to do. 'Divine Truth' comes to them through ____ leaves! Longing after idols has made them foolish" (Hos. 4:12)

ACROSS

1 Sarah's response upon hearing she would have a son in her old age (Gen. 18:12)
5 "A short-tempered man must bear his own penalty; you can't do much to help him. If you try once you must try a ____ times"; number (Pro. 19:19)
8 Commander of King David's Sixth Division (1 Ch. 27:9)
9 Ornamental borders of clothes (Mk. 6:56)
10 Famous warrior joining David at Ziklag (1 Ch. 11:44)
11 "Martha was the jittery ____ and was worrying over the big dinner she was preparing" (Luk. 10:40)
12 "Crafty men are caught in their own traps; God thwarts their ____"; stratagems (Job 5:12, 13)
14 Kind of altar outside the Tabernacle: 2 wds. (Exo. 30:28)
15 Condition of being secluded (Joe. 2:16)
18 Famous warrior among David's men (1 Ch. 11:26, 29)
21 Break without completely separating (1 Ki. 13:5)
22 Distributed as a share (Eze. 48:21)
23 "____ father was Joshua" (Luk. 3:29)
24 Moved away from fright (Num. 22:33)
25 Blocks or defeats (Job 5:13)

DOWN

1 "Anyone who listens to my message and believes in God who sent me has eternal ____, and will never be damned for his sins" (Joh. 5:24)
2 Make into a coherent whole (Eze. 37:22)
3 Placed at top, such as military officers: 2 wds. (1 Ch. 27:6)
4 Computer floppies
5 Relationship of Ruth to Naomi (8-2-3; Rut. 4:15)
6 Tribe of giants conquered by King Chedorlaomer (Gen. 14:5)
7 "When I return the world will be as indifferent to the things of God as the people were in ____ day" (Luk. 17:26)
11 "There is no ____ statement than this: God is never wicked or unjust"; more genuine (Job 34:12)
13 Boredom
15 Compact groups (Hos. 6:9)
16 Inhabitant of country from which Abraham came (Act. 7:2)
17 Leavening agent forbidden during Passover (Exo. 12:19)
19 Elevated structure for religious ceremonies (Gen. 8:20)
20 "The people of the Lord marched down against great ____"; probabilities (Jdg. 5:13)

PUZZLE 24

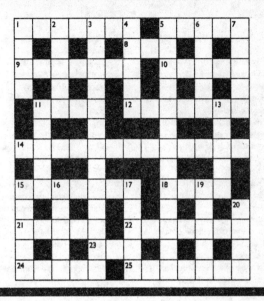

ACROSS

1 Break up an organization (1 Ki. 12:24)
5 Direction on your left when facing east (Gen. 13:1)
8 "Bring to [the Lord] a free-will offering _____ in size to his blessing upon you"; commensurate (Deu. 16:10)
9 "Make use of the Light while there is still time; then you will become light _____"; carriers (Joh. 12:36)
11 Head cook (1 Sa. 9:24)
15 Murder for political reasons (Est. 7:9)
17 "Lord, _____ me as you promised me you would. Tell me clearly what to do, which way to turn" (Psa. 5:8)
19 Fast gaits of horses (Eze. 26:10)
22 Severe criticisms (Mat. 11:20)
24 Men (Lev. 7:6)
25 Sons of a brother or sister (2 Ch. 22:8)

DOWN

1 What Judas does with disciples' funds for his own use (Joh. 12:6)
2 Digging tools (Num. 21:18)
3 Fuss or bother
4 Resolution (Act. 3:13)
5 Corner or private place (Luk. 15:8)
6 "Stay always within the boundaries where God's love can _____ and bless you"; extend to (Jud. 1:21)
7 Cultivate (Isa. 5:6)
10 "It is foolish and _____ to make a promise to the Lord before counting the cost"; prematurely hasty (Pro. 20:25)
12 "As for others, help them to _____ the Lord by being kind to them"; discover (Jud. 1:23)
13 Missionary to the Gentiles (Eph. 3:1)
14 "Seek the Lord while you can find him. _____ upon him now while he is near" (Isa. 55:6)
16 "Pray for the happiness of those who curse you; _____ God's blessing on those who hurt you." (Luk. 6:28)
18 Cancel (Eph. 2:15)
20 "Before every man there lies a wide and pleasant road that seems right but _____ in death"; terminates (Pro. 14:12)
21 "If God decides to argue with him, can a man answer even one question of a thousand he _____?" (Job 9:3)
22 Watercourse barrier (Ecc. 1:15)
23 "Finally, the innocent shall come out on _____, above the godless" (Job 17:8)

PUZZLE 25

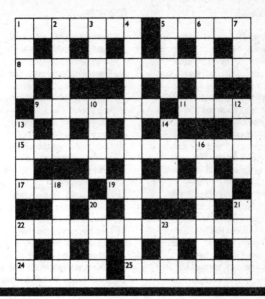

51

ACROSS

1 "Everyone who asks, receives; and the door is opened to everyone who ____" (Luk. 11:10)
5 Crystal clear; transparent, as a pool of water (Sg. 7:4)
8 Wedding vow response: 2 wds.
9 "To ____ these gifts, you need more than faith; you must also work hard to be good" (2 Pe. 1:5)
10 "Receive the love he ____ you—be reconciled to God" (2 Co. 5:20)
11 Allot; deal out (Eze. 23:45)
12 Freed from some liability or responsibility (1 Sa. 17:25)
14 Quote from Psa. 100:2; an invitation from God: 3 wds.
17 John the Baptist "will ____ many a Jew to turn to the Lord his God" (Luk. 1:16)
19 "He traded his rights as the oldest son for a single meal" (Heb. 12:16)
21 Have high regard for (Luk. 16:8)
23 "All who ____ a blessing or take an oath shall swear by the God of Truth" (Isa. 65:16)
24 "The rivers of God will not ____ dry" (Psa. 65:9)
25 "When you fast, put on festive clothing, so that no one will suspect you are hungry, except your Father who knows every ____" (Mat. 6:17, 18)
26 Poured forth violently (Job 38:8)

DOWN

2 Aristocratic; of high and stately character, such as the name of Christ (Jam. 2:7)
3 Continuous; without stopping (Ecc. 8:16)
4 Genuine; without hypocrisy, such as a prayer (Psa. 143:8)
5 Set free from restraint; not fixed (Jer. 50:6)
6 Foreign evangelistic support service organization: abbr.
7 Citizen of Hebrews' homeland (Num. 15:30)
13 "The Lord ____ the upright but ruins the plans of the wicked" (Pro. 22:12)
15 Late; past expected time (Hab. 2:3)
16 "If our consciences are clear, we can come to the Lord with perfect assurance and trust, and get whatever we ask for because we are ____ him" (1 Jo. 3:21, 22)
18 "Keep ____ and pray. Otherwise temptation will overpower you" (Mat. 26:41)
20 Foot-leg joint (Act. 3:7)
22 Part of aerial guidance system: abbr.

ACROSS

1 "They will come to their ____ and escape from Satan's trap of slavery to sin" (2 Ti. 2:26)

5 "Some will come to me—those the Father has given me—and I will never, never ____ them" (Joh. 6:37)

8 "____ that your hearts do not turn from God to worship other gods" (Deu. 11:16)

9 Placing; putting (Lev. 16:21)

10 "The love of money is the first ____ toward all kinds of sin" (I Ti. 6:10)

11 Deliberate act of deception (Act. 13:10)

13 Quote from Psalm 100:2 about our response to God: 3 wds.

16 "We patiently endure suffering and ____ and trouble of every kind" (2 Co. 6:4)

18 "A man will always reap just the kind of crop he ____" (Gal. 6:7)

20 Winner in a battle or contest (Zec. 9:9)

22 Free, open right of entry (Mat. 18:10)

23 Shocked, as by something terrible; appalled (Nah. 2:10)

24 Make sure or certain (Deu. 17:20)

DOWN

2 Choose by vote (2 Sa. 3:21)

3 "Wisdom is hid from the eyes of all mankind; even the ____ birds in the sky cannot discover it" (Job 28:21)

4 Distinctive odor (Sg. 4:11)

5 "Having started the ball ____ so enthusiastically, you should carry this project through to completion just as gladly" (2 Co. 8:11)

6 "When the Holy Spirit controls our lives he will produce this kind of fruit in us: love, ____, peace" (Gal. 5:22)

7 "Anyone who says he is a Christian but doesn't ____ his sharp tongue is just fooling himself" (Jam. 1:26)

12 Strapped, back bag to carry supplies: pl. (Mk. 6:8)

14 "They are like trees along a river bank ____ luscious fruit" (Psa. 1:3)

15 Come into possession by legal succession (Luk. 20:14)

17 "I am leaving you with a gift—____ of mind and heart" (Joh. 14:27)

19 "Your words make me ____ than my enemies because they are my constant guide" (Psa. 119:96, 98)

21 Beverage made by steeping dried leaves in boiling water (Hos. 4:12)

ACROSS

1 Pour forth; spill (Gen. 37:22)
5 Gentle blow
8 Obtains (Num. 31:28)
12 Hillside hollow (Gen. 19:30)
13 Hole maker (Exo. 21:6)
14 Yearn (2 Co. 6:10)
15 "I don't give ____": slang: 2 wds
16 Perceive (Gen. 2:19)
17 National Collegiate Athletic Association: abbr.
18 Soften; mellow (Hos. 13:14)
20 Earnest; determined (Mat. 11:12)
22 Never: Ger.
23 Measure
24 Hebrews' departure from Egypt
27 Fit to be eaten (Mat. 13:48)
31 ____ Dodds (Christian athlete)
32 Sound receptacle (Psa. 80:1)
33 Hebrew returnee from Babylon (Ezr. 2:55, 56)
37 Security (Gen. 38:17)
40 Gorilla or gibbon, e.g. (1 Ki. 10:22)
41 Make a mistake
42 Levite; Temple gatekeeper (1 Ch. 9:17)
45 From one side to other (Gen. 2:11)
49 Costa ____
50 Town of Israel (2 Ki. 9:27)
52 First shepherd (Gen. 4:2)
53 "Am I ____," Goliath roared: 2 wds. (1 Sa. 17:43)
54 Hand clapping
55 Moses' death site (Deu. 34:1, 5)
56 ____ jaakan, wilderness site (Num. 33:31)
57 Daily time indicators: abbr.
58 Dull; plain

DOWN

1 Disease or injury mark (Lev. 13:23)
2 Large rabbit
3 Bad; wicked (Gen. 3:5)
4 "We ____ upon the Lord alone to save us" (Psa. 33:20)
5 Senses flavor (Pro. 23:2)
6 Reverence and wonder (Deu. 28:10)
7 Satisfy; give pleasure (Exo. 21:8)
8 Mahatma ____ (Indian leader)
9 "____ homo"
10 Comparison term (Gen. 25:23)
11 Sitting spot (Lev. 15:6)
19 Northern Illinois University: abbr.
21 Energy unit
24 Hen's product (Job 6:6)
25 Roman twelve
26 Specified age (Gen. 5:3)
28 Sleeping place (Gen. 47:31)
29 Fall behind (Deu. 25:18)
30 Prior
34 Harm; loss (Est. 7:4)
35 Environmental Protection Agency: abbr.
36 Measured distance (Exo. 26:12)
37 Oyster's gems (Mat. 13:46)
38 Learning Resource Center: abbr.
39 Short, specific mission (1 Sa. 15:18)
42 Semitic person; not a Jew (Neh. 2:19)
43 Keep undisclosed (Gen. 18:17)
44 Image symbol
46 ____ ammergau, Passion Play site
47 Son of Cush (Gen. 10:7)
48 Crude or unkempt person: infor.
51 United Arab Republic: abbr.

ACROSS

1 Son of Benjamin (Gen. 46:21)
4 Unenclosed (Lev. 14:53)
8 David's military head (2 Sa. 2:13)
12 Fish eggs
13 "Take ____ of yourself" (Jam. 2:8)
14 Confined by: abbr. (Exo. 27:9)
15 Mine
16 Rounded handle
17 Covers with tears (Psa. 6:6)
18 Signer of Nehemiah's covenant (Neh. 10:16)
20 "The voice is Jacob's, but the hands are ____" (Gen. 27:22)
22 Drinking glasses with stem (1 Ki. 7:26)
24 Duct
27 Loathe (Lev. 20:23)
29 Blot out (Psa. 51:9)
31 "Oh, that you were ____ proud!": 2 wds. (Jer. 13:15)
32 Roman governor trying Paul (Act. 23:24)
33 Healthy; thriving (Gen. 41:2)
34 Join together as one (Jdg. 20:11)
35 Increase (Lev. 27:31)
36 Southern Judean town (Jos. 15:21, 30)
40 Forceful, noisy breathing (Job 39:25)
41 Research places: infor.
44 Intertwined (Lam. 1:14)
47 Good-bye
49 ____ o'-shanter
50 Arabian prince
51 Mastered
52 Old French coin
53 Lowest part of lampstand (Exo. 25:31)
54 First-century Roman emperor
55 ____ Hammarskjold (U.N. secy-gen.)

DOWN

1 Kiriath ____ (Judean city also called Hebron)
2 Vehicle passageway (Gen. 16:7)
3 Took great pleasure in (Lk. 23:8)
4 Weight
5 Flat wall portion (1 Ki. 7:31)
6 Irregular; uneven
7 Jeroboam's father (1 Ki. 11:26)
8 Hebrews (Ezr. 1:3)
9 A single (Gen. 2:21)
10 "Don't try to ____ big" (Rom. 12:16)
11 Large stone squares: abbr. (1 Ki. 5:17)
19 Rope-loop trap (Job 41:1)
21 "The whole Bible was given to us by inspiration from God and is ____ to teach us" (2 Ti. 3:16)
23 Shattered (Lev. 6:28)
24 Legally substantiated
25 Jesus acted ____ he were going farther: 2 wds. (Luk. 24:28)
26 Arousing passions
27 Advanced network systems architecture: computer abbr.
28 Daring (Jos. 1:9)
30 Related to kidneys
37 Horite chief (Gen. 36:22)
38 Visible evidence (Exo. 17:14)
39 Aquatic mammal
40 Withered (Psa. 129:6)
42 Valley in Palestine (Psa. 84:6; KJV)
43 Self-satisfied
44 Spider's trap (Job 8:14)
45 Airline code for major Nebraska city
46 Force; power
48 Fuss; trouble

PUZZLE 29

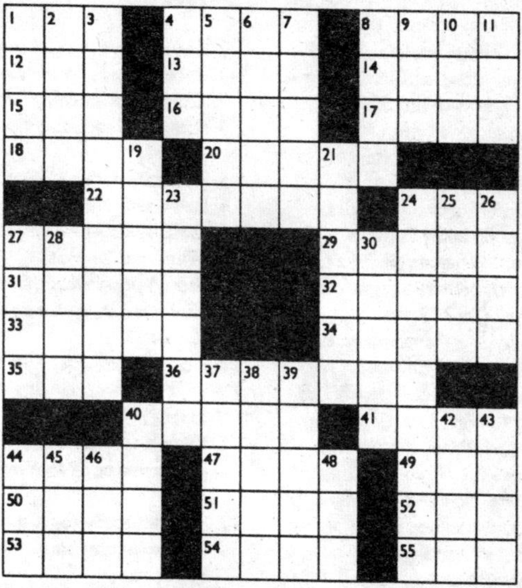

ACROSS

1 Angel; Persian city (Ezr. 2:59)
5 Prophet Moabites hired to curse the Israelites (Num. 22:5-7)
8 "This truth was given me in secret, as though whispered in my ____" (Job 4:12)
9 Small compartment for clothes storage (1 Sa. 21:9)
10 "Cursed is he who is unjust to the foreigner, the ____, and the widow" (Deu. 27:19)
11 "We can ____ anything as long as we know that you remain strong in the Lord"; endure (1 Th. 3:8)
12 "God tolerated man's past ignorance about these things, but now he ____ everyone to put away idols and worship only him"; orders (Act. 17:30)
14 "Anxious hearts are very heavy, but a word of ____ does wonders" (Pro. 12:25)
18 Soldiers' housing (Phi. 1:13)
20 "A lazy fellow has trouble all through life; the good man's path is ____"; free from difficulty (Pro. 15:19)
22 "You get no credit for being patient if you are ____ for doing wrong"; punished with blows (1 Pe. 2:20)
24 "Christ is the exact likeness of the ____ God"; invisible (Col. 1:15)
25 "Satan, the mighty prince of the power of the ____" (Eph. 2:2)
26 Walk leisurely (2 Sa. 11:2)
27 Belonging to the country holding Hebrews for 400 years (Exo. 14:7)

DOWN

2 Cut into two parts (Gen. 15:10)
3 Place to store liquid (Zec. 4:3)
4 City Philistines fled to when scared by God's thunder (1 Sa. 7:10, 11)
5 Flowering shrub (1 Ki. 19:4)
6 Level part of a seated person (2 Ki. 4:20)
7 "The Lord will not ____ his chosen people, for that would dishonor his great name"; desert (1 Sa. 12:22)
11 Honey maker (Psa. 118:12)
13 Without direction or a goal (Gen. 21:14)
15 Closest (Mat. 8:33)
16 Expressive body movement (Deu. 12:6)
17 "Work happily together. Don't ____ to act big"; attempt (Rom. 12:16)
19 Man-made waterway (Eze. 1:1)
21 Distinctive odor (Sg. 4:11)
23 Also (Gen. 3:6)

ACROSS

1 Eye cosmetic (Jer. 4:30)
5 Engaged in, such as war (Rev. 17:14)
8 "Learn to be wise ... and develop good judgment and common sense! I cannot _____ this point"; stress too much (Pro. 4:5)
9 Position, such as an army (2 Ch. 33:14)
11 "May those curses return and cling to him like his clothing or his _____"; waistband (Psa. 109:19)
15 Lacking self-control
17 Weeps aloud with convulsive gasping (Gen. 27:34)
19 Breaks up plowed soil before planting (Hos. 10:11)
22 "When you hear of wars and _____ beginning, don't panic.... The end won't follow immediately"; revolutions (Luk. 21:9)
24 "The man _____ his wife Eve (meaning 'The life-giving one')" (Gen. 3:20)
25 Longed for with an aching (Isa. 62:1)

DOWN

1 State of mind or emotion (Joh. 7:32)
2 Filled with an odor (Sg. 5:13)
3 "You _____ the world's seasoning, to make it tolerable" (Mat. 5:13)
4 Nearly correct (Jos. 7:4)
5 "My power shows up best in _____ people"; lacking vigor (2 Co. 12:9)
6 "We _____ along the tides of time as swiftly as a racing river, and vanish as quickly as a dream"; move smoothly (Psa. 90:5)
7 "In _____ season Christ will be revealed from heaven by the blessed and only Almighty God"; appropriate (1 Ti. 6:15)
10 "We beg you not to _____ aside this marvelous message of God's great kindness"; cast (2 Co. 6:1)
12 Be enough to allow one to get by for a time (Heb. 9:10)
13 Partly-opened flowers that developed on Aaron's rod (Num. 17:5)
14 Aspersion (Gen. 30:23)
16 Neonatal infant (Exo. 1:22)
18 "We should behave like God's very own children, adopted into the _____ of his family, and calling to him, 'Father, Father'"; heart (Rom. 8:15)
20 Stepped upon (Rev. 19:15)
21 "Do not let any part of your bodies become tools of wickedness, to be _____ for sinning" (Rom. 6:13)
22 The Hebrew spies stayed at an _____ operated by Rahab (Jos. 2:1)
23 Beverage made by steeping shrub leaves (Hos. 4:12)

ACROSS

1 Having a full, rounded form (Eze. 34:22)
4 "Laziness lets the roof leak, and soon the _____ begin to rot"; roof supports (Ecc. 10:18)
8 "Give generously, for your gifts will return to you _____"; at a subsequent time (Ecc. 11:1)
9 Nomadic Arab (Jer. 3:2)
10 Unauthorized entry; illegal act (Eze. 46:20)
11 "What a glorious Lord! He who daily bears our burdens _____ gives us our salvation"; in addition (Psa. 68:19)
13 "The Lord is close to those whose hearts are breaking; he rescues those who are humbly _____ for their sins"; regretful (Psa. 34:18)
15 Female servants (Mk. 14:66)
19 Excessively dry
20 Close relationship (Ezr. 9:14; KJV)
23 Extreme (Act. 22:11)
24 O.T. prophet who married a prostitute
25 "You have _____ him with eternal happiness. You have given him the unquenchable joy of your presence"; furnished (Psa. 21:6)
26 Abysses (Jer. 16:16)

DOWN

1 Roman official who authorized Jesus' execution (Mat. 27:24)
2 "Don't you _____ your cattle from their stalls on the Sabbath and lead them out for water?" loose (Luk. 13:15)
3 Sweat (Eze. 44:18)
4 "The child Jesus became a strong, _____ lad, and was known for wisdom beyond his years; and God poured out his blessings on him"; vigorously healthy (Luk. 2:40)
5 "Our natural lives will _____ as grass does when it becomes all brown and dry"; wither (1 Pe. 1:24)
6 "At God's command Moses performed amazing miracles that have never been _____"; duplicated or rivaled (Deu. 34:11)
7 Older or higher-ranking (Gen. 50:7)
12 Starved for food (Gen. 41:55; KJV)
14 Left out (2 Ch. 21:19)
16 Steep-sided valley (Joh. 18:1)
17 Hurt or insult (Joh. 6:61)
18 Side roads (Jdg. 5:6; KJV)
21 "'Woe to unjust judges and to those who _____ unfair laws,' says the Lord"; pass down (Isa. 10:1)
22 "In this way each generation has been able to obey his laws and to set its hope _____ on God and not forget his glorious miracles"; over again (Psa. 78:7)

ACROSS

1 "He asked them, 'Who do you think I am?' Peter replied, 'The Messiah—the ____ of God!'" (Luk. 9:20)
5 Deliver a sermon (Jon. 3:4)
8 "The days will come when all who ____ a blessing or take an oath shall swear by the God of Truth" (Isa. 65:16)
9 "No one needed to tell him how changeable human ____ is!" (Joh. 2:24)
10 Admin's father (in Jesus' family tree; Luk. 3:33)
11 Something taught or believed (1 Ti. 1:3)
12 Island where John wrote the Book of Revelation (Rev. 1:9)
14 "Act in a way ____ of those who have been chosen for such wonderful blessings" (Eph. 4:1)
16 "God publicly endorsed Jesus of Nazareth by doing tremendous ____ through him" (Act. 2:22)
19 "Honor your marriage and its ____, and be pure" (Heb. 13:4)
21 Syrian false god (2 Ki. 5:17, 18)
22 Commit money to another in hopes of a profit (Luk. 19:13)
23 Large Mediterranean island near Syria (Act. 21:3)
24 City of homeless, demon-possessed man Jesus healed (Luk. 8:27)

DOWN

2 "If you ____ your father and mother, yours will be a long life" (Eph. 6:3)
3 City near Antioch and Lystra where Paul preached (2 Ti. 3:11)
4 Insurrection leader killed by the Romans (Act. 5:36)
5 "When you hear of wars and insurrections beginning, don't ____. The end won't follow immediately" (Luk. 21:9)
6 "This was his riddle: 'Food came out of the ____, and sweetness from the strong'" (Jdg. 14:14)
7 Home city of Aquila and Priscilla (Act. 18:1, 2)
13 "God has given each of us the ____ to do certain things well" (Rom. 12:6)
14 "Master, you shouldn't be ____ our feet like this" (Joh. 13:6)
15 "Onesiphorus' visits ____ me like a breath of fresh air" (2 Ti. 1:16)
17 "Use every piece of God's ____ to resist the enemy whenever he attacks" (Eph. 6:13)
18 "Eubulus sends you greetings, and so do Pudens, ____, Claudia, and all the others" (2 Ti. 4:21)
20 Solomon was ____ than any other man

ACROSS

1 Small place of worship (Amo. 7:13)
5 "There's no use arguing with a fool. He only rages and _____, and tempers flare"; mocks (Pro. 29:9)
8 An official of King Solomon (Ezr. 2:55, 57)
9 Short trip for specific task (Jer. 47:7)
10 Prophet who confronted David regarding Bathsheba (2 Sa. 12:13)
11 Main seaport of Syria (Act. 21:3)
12 After tenth (Num. 7:72)
14 Confidence in oneself (Isa. 3:18)
17 Swelled out in rolling waves (Exo. 19:18)
19 "It is hard to stop a quarrel _____ it starts, so don't let it begin"; after (Pro. 17:14)
21 "I will _____ all peoples of the earth, including my people in Israel, and he shall bring peace among the nations"; remove weapons from (Zec. 9:10)
23 One who understands written words (Mk. 13:14)
24 "Since your real home is in heaven, I _____ you to keep away from the evil pleasures of this world"; plead (1 Pe. 2:11)
25 Offensive; hateful; abhorrent (Pro. 30:23; KJV)
26 "Thank God that though you once chose to be slaves of sin, now you have _____ with all your heart the teaching to which God has committed you"; followed (Rom. 6:17)

DOWN

2 "Never be in a _____ about choosing a pastor"; rush (1 Ti. 5:22)
3 "Be glad for all God is planning for you. Be patient in trouble, and _____ always"; inclined to talk with God (Rom. 12:12)
4 Devices with rungs for climbing (Deu. 20:20)
5 "_____ God loved us as much as that, we surely ought to love each other too"; because (1 Jo. 4:11)
6 "This cup is the new testament in my blood: this do ye, as _____ as ye drink it, in remembrance of me"; frequently (1 Co. 11:25; KJV)
7 Wildly excited (Act. 5:24)
13 Complex and ornate (Exo. 39:5)
15 Built up spiritually (Act. 9:31; KJV)
16 "God will tenderly comfort you when you _____ these same sufferings"; endure; pass through (2 Co. 1:7)
18 Places of earliest stages of development (Hos. 9:14)
20 Mediterranean island where Titus ministered (Tit. 1:5)
22 Fuss (Mk. 5:39; KJV)

68

ACROSS

1 Atmosphere (2 Sa. 16:13)
4 Respectful address to Indian: var.
8 To cover with icing
12 Southeastern U.S. state: abbr.
13 "Christ is the ____ of his body, the Church" (Eph. 4:15)
14 Italian city
15 Southern Judean city (Jos. 15:21, 32)
16 Energized; authorized (Luk. 11:19)
18 An Ethiopian prince
19 Smoked salmon
20 Up to date with (Pro. 24:3)
25 Married
28 Narrate the facts (Heb. 11:32)
30 Fodder (1 Co. 3:12)
31 Command from God: 3 wds. (quote excepted from Joh. 16:24)
35 ____ West
36 Broke from captivity (Gen. 14:13)
37 Assembled listeners: abbr. (Act. 25:24)
38 Prepared again for a task (2 Ti. 3:17)
40 Atomic Energy Commission: abbr.
41 Son of Caleb (1 Ch. 4:15)
44 David's wife; Solomon's mother (1 Ki. 1:11)
50 Constantly complain (Jdg. 16:16)
51 Body fluid compound
52 King of Israel (1 Ki. 16:8)
53 Green indicator lamp: abbr.
54 Name of rock and winepress (Jdg. 7:25)
55 Dyansen Corp. trademark
56 Cunning

DOWN

1 Long distance away (Isa 30:27)
2 Pelvis bones
3 Pillaged (1 Ki. 14:26)
4 Her (Gen. 3:20)
5 Garment's folded edge (1 Sa. 24:11)
6 Talk freely and frankly
7 Worship images (Gen. 31:30)
8 Goat (Deu. 14:5)
9 Beth____ (1 Sa. 7:11)
10 Before
11 ____ Caesar
17 Know of
21 ____ constrictor
22 Operate steadily (Gen. 39:5)
23 Final extent (Gen. 9:13)
24 "Anyone who is hanged on ____ is cursed": 2 wds. (Gal. 3:13)
25 Repeated lashings (Gal. 6:17)
26 "Don't ____sdrop!" (Ecc. 7:21)
27 Changed color (Exo. 39:34)
28 ____h; baby massacre site (Mat. 2:18)
29 Birthright trader (Heb. 12:16)
32 Male courtesy title: abbr.
33 Coronary care unit: abbr.
34 Education Auditing Institute: abbr.
38 Follows do musically: pl.
39 Enlarged: obs.
40 King Omri's son (1 Ki. 16:28)
42 Hurl insults (1 Sa. 25:14)
43 Not pretty
44 Nephew of Abraham (Gen. 22:20, 21)
45 "Humble men ____ very fortunate!" (Mat. 5:3)
46 Golf ball holder
47 Easterly: abbr.
48 Sheepish announcement?
49 Army health nurse: abbr.

PUZZLE 35

1
2
3
4
5
6
7
8
9
10
11
12
13
14
15
16
17
18
19
20
21
22
23
24
25
26
27
28
29
30
31
32
33
34
35
36
37
38
39
40
41
42
43
44
45
46
47
48
49
50
51
52
53
54
55
56

ACROSS

1 Joab's brother, who could run like a deer in battle (2 Sa. 2:18)
5 King who rid Israel of Jezebel and Baal worship (2 Ki. 10:19, 20)
9 Curved seizing and holding devices used to capture King Manasseh (2 Ch. 33:10, 11)
10 Marches, as in a procession (Lk. 20:46)
11 Liquid containers Gideon's army used to conceal their torches (Jdg. 7:19; KJV)
13 Extended travel on an assignment (Num. 13:25)
15 Pack animal; offspring between donkey and horse (2 Sa. 18:9)
16 Two-wheeled hauling device, often pulled by animals (1 Sa. 6:7)
20 Shallow stream crossing site (Gen. 32:22)
21 "Some nations boast of armies and of _____, but our boast is in the Lord our God"; implements of war (Psa. 20:7)
24 Tribe of Israel; enemy of Judah (Isa. 9:21)
25 One of 12 spies; man in tribe of Benjamin (Num. 13:3, 9)
26 "God sometimes _____ sorrow in our lives to help us turn away from sin and seek eternal life"; employs (2 Co. 7:10)
27 Intense desire for liquid (Exo. 15:24)

DOWN

2 "Select three men from each tribe, and I will send them to _____ the unconquered territory and bring back a report of its size and natural divisions so that I can divide it for you" (Jos. 18:4)
3 Posesses
4 "Ten _____ stood at a distance, crying out, 'Jesus, sir, have mercy on us'" (Luk. 17:12, 13)
5 What Gideon's army broke so their torches blazed in the night (Jdg. 7:19)
6 Place to remain out of sight (1 Sa. 20:19)
7 Large water navigation crafts (Gen. 49:13)
8 Seize and hold without right (Ecc. 4:15)
12 Sword handle (Jdg. 3:22)
14 Temporary army quarters (1 Sa. 26:5)
15 "Though a mighty army _____ against me, my heart shall know no fear! I am confident that God will save me" (Psa. 27:3)
17 Present for acceptance (Psa. 4:5)
18 Protective covering for a soldier's head (1 Sa. 17:38)
19 King of Persia who conquered Babylon and freed the captive Jews (2 Ch. 36:22)
22 Back of the neck: pl.
23 Armed conflict between nations (2 Sa. 7:11)
25 A loyalist to King David (1 Ki. 1:8)

PUZZLE 36

ACROSS

1 "Noah's ____ in God was in direct contrast to the rest of the world"; trust (Heb. 11:7)

5 Harmonious notes sounded together (Isa. 24:8)

8 Implement to propel a boat (Eze. 27:6)

9 "In that day he who created the royal dynasty of David will be a ____ of salvation to all the world"; flag or standard (Isa. 11:10)

10 Not readily controlled or disciplined (Exo. 33:5)

11 "____ friends, never avenge yourselves. Leave that to God"; highly valued (Rom. 12:19)

12 Years of rest for the Hebrews' land (Lev. 26:35)

14 Admitting something's true (1 Ki. 1:47)

17 Seemed desirable (1 Sa. 15:9)

19 "God has given ____ of you some special abilities; be sure to use them to help ____ other" (1 Pe. 4:10)

21 "I have had to feed you with milk and not with solid food because you couldn't ____ anything stronger"; assimilate (1 Co. 3:2)

23 "It is ____ for a camel to go through the eye of a needle than for a rich man to enter the Kingdom of God"; less difficult (Mk. 10:25)

24 "My purpose is to give life in all ____ fullness (Joh. 10:10)

25 Pattern or sketch (Num. 8:4)

26 Angelic creature that serves and worships God in heaven

DOWN

2 Manage to escape (Jer. 25:29)

3 "If anyone thinks he knows all the answers, he is just showing his ____"; lack of knowledge (1 Co. 8:2)

4 Realized ahead of time; anticipated (Pro. 22:3)

5 Small fragment (Amo. 5:11)

6 "If we confess ____ sins to God, he can be depended on to forgive us and to cleanse us from every wrong" (1 Jo. 1:9)

7 Trainable sea mammal (Eze. 16:9)

13 One who makes an unprovoked attack

15 Prisoner (Zec. 1:14)

16 "I was the one chosen for this special joy of telling the Gentiles the Glad News of the ____ treasures available to them in Christ"; unlimited (Eph. 3:8)

18 Language of ancient Romans (Joh. 19:20)

20 "Silver was too ____ to count for much in those days"; inexpensive (2 Ch. 9:20)

22 Father of Hophni and Phinehas (1 Sa. 1:3)

ACROSS

1 Carved pole used as tribal emblem or idol (Eze. 43:9)
4 Hung to swing freely, such as Absalom by his hair (2 Sa. 18:14)
8 Equal Rights Amendment: abbr.
9 Engaged in regularly; exercised diligently (Luk. 11:53)
10 Living without a permanent home (Jer. 25:24)
11 One who carves letters in stone or metal (2 Ch. 2:14)
12 The Jewish leaders "could think of nothing, for Jesus was a ____ to the people—they hung on every word he said" (Luk. 19:48)
14 Private teacher (1 Ch. 27:32)
16 Group of civilians aiding law enforcement (2 Ki. 21:24)
20 Speed contest (1 Co. 9:24)
21 Shook; spoke with trembling (1 Sa. 22:12)
24 Player of a pipelike musical instrument (Isa. 30:29)
25 Jewish religious leader and teacher (Mat. 9:18)
26 Likely; suitable (Exo. 34:15)
27 "The Jewish leaders were surprised when they heard Jesus. 'How can he know so much when he's never been to our ____?' they asked" (Joh. 7:15)
28 "O Belteshazzar, I know that the spirit of the holy gods is in you and no mystery is too great for you to ____" (Dan. 4:9)

DOWN

1 Having point covered or extended, such as a spear (1 Sa. 17:7)
2 Fastening together, such as with cord or ribbon (Exo. 39:21)
3 "Moses was the go-between—the ____ between the people of Israel and the Angel who gave them the Law of God" (Act. 7:38)
4 Moved rhythmically to music (Mk. 6:22)
5 "God raised Jesus up to the heights of heaven and gave him a ____ which is above every other" (Phi. 2:9)
6 Runged climbing devices (Deu. 20:20)
7 Luke's occupation (Col. 4:14)
13 "Some who listened were persuaded and became ____"; new believers (Act. 17:4)
15 Rude and vulgar, like Nabal (1 Sa. 25:3)
17 Occupations requiring special skills (Exo. 35:35)
18 Production allotments; assigned minimums (Exo. 5:14)
19 Have high regard for (Luk. 16:8)
22 "It is senseless to pay tuition to educate a ____ who has no heart for truth"; one who resists authority (Pro. 17:16)
23 Home of one of David's top thirty soldiers (2 Sa. 23:34)

76

ACROSS

1 Instrumental group (2 Ch. 5:13)
5 Large tub (1 Ki. 7:38)
8 Restrain or moderate
12 Spice used on Jesus' body (Joh. 19:39)
13 Piercing site (Exo. 21:6)
14 Hushai's father (1 Ch. 7:12)
15 Mourn (2 Sa. 1:24)
16 Woman: pron. (Gen. 2:23)
17 Circular jewelry (Gen. 41:41)
18 Hold-ups (Eze. 12:25)
20 Belonging to Miriam's brother (Exo. 15:20)
22 ___ vs. Wade
23 Particular
24 Door beam (Exo. 12:22)
27 Jerked (Jdg. 16:14)
31 African or Asian people
32 Independent retirement account: abbr.
33 Prepare for burial (Luk. 23:56)
37 Stray (2 Jo. 1:9)
40 Round, green vegetable (Gen. 25:34)
41 Industry standard architecture: computer abbr.
42 Defense device (Jdg. 14:6)
45 Son of Cush (Gen. 10:7)
49 Eve's second child (Gen. 4:2)
50 Son of Leah and Jacob (Gen. 30:11)
52 Greasy; slick (Psa. 55:21)
53 Stab with a horn (Exo. 21:29)
54 Bible's second book: abbr.
55 Capture device (Jos. 8:22)
56 Grandson of Adam and Eve (Luk. 3:38)
57 Programming comment: computer abbr.
58 Present place (Gen. 13:9)

DOWN

1 Prostitute
2 Away from the wind
3 "The first ___, the angels did say"
4 Leave (1 Jo. 2:27)
5 Large boat (Eze. 27:26)
6 Ooh and ___
7 Covenant; agreement (Gen. 26:28)
8 Childless (Gen. 11:30)
9 Abinadab's son (2 Sa. 6:3)
10 Eastern U.S. state: abbr.
11 Dyne's worth of energy units
19 Ye Olde Enoch: abbr.
21 Expression of surprise or triumph (Job 39:25)
24 Strong cleaning acid (Job 9:30)
25 "Just say, '___' has sent me" (Exo. 3:14)
26 Home town of Ahimelech, the priest (1 Sa. 21:1)
28 Child: slang (1 Sa. 17:33)
29 Before
30 Daughters of the American Revolution: abbr.
34 Hard, often red-skinned fruit (Pro. 9:17)
35 Northern hemisphere constellation
36 Animals' feeding trough (Luk. 2:7)
37 Common sense; decision-making insight (Pro. 2:1)
38 Photographic film speed rating: abbr.
39 Vineyard owner Jezebel killed (1 Ki. 21:15)
42 Pay (Deu. 24:15)
43 Teak wood: arch. (Eze. 27:15)
44 Related to aircraft: pref.
46 Grow weary (Pro. 30:2)
47 Controversial chemical sprayed on fruit
48 Advertising claims
51 Woodchopping tool (Deu. 19:5)

ACROSS

1 Double-cross; sell out (Jos. 2:14)
7 Thin, crisp crackers (Lev. 2:4)
13 "Beautiful bdellium and even lapis _____" (Gen. 2:12)
14 N.T. name for Edom (Mk. 3:8)
15 Suitable for growing crops
16 Designating (Zec. 11:7)
17 Not genuine
18 Subject matters (Mat. 3:1)
19 Job's wife said, "Curse him and _____" (Job 2:9)
20 Miniature representations (1 Sa. 6:17)
25 Clatter in rapid succession (Job 39:23)
31 Humble; degrade
32 Bundle of grain stalks (Gen. 37:7)
33 One who owes something (Jer. 15:10)
35 Digits opposed to four (Lam. 5:12)
36 Self-esteem
37 "A _____ goes around spreading rumors" (Pro. 11:13)
42 King of Israel; enemy of Judah (1 Ki. 15:16)
48 Layman living in a monastery
49 City of Manasseh (Jos. 17:11)
50 Dried grape (1 Sa. 25:18)
51 Burning
52 Levites replaced all the _____ sons of Israel (Num. 8:18)
53 Hurry (Job 20:2)

DOWN

1 Blue: Ger.
2 Deserve (Rom. 4:4)
3 Russian ruler before 1917
4 Awkward, unsophisticated person
5 _____ breve (musical notation)
6 Produces; bears (Psa. 85:12)
7 Season between autumn and spring (Pro. 6:8)
8 One of Esau's wives (Gen. 36:2)
9 Boil up; rage (1 Sa. 20:3)
10 Giant inhabitants of plain of Kiriathaim (Gen. 14:5)
11 _____ Pache, European theologian and author
12 Droops
20 Crazy (2 Co. 11:23)
21 Ancient Laconian clan
22 Apply lightly
23 Calculate approximately: abbr. (2 Ki. 25:16)
24 Fifth sign of zodiac
26 Combustion debris (Jer. 52:18)
27 Fifth day of week: abbr.
28 Not permanent: abbr. (1 Ki. 8:64)
29 Experimental site
30 Sixth letter: pl.
34 "He is giving more time for sinners to _____" (2 Pe. 3:9)
35 Samaritan opposed to Nehemiah (Neh. 6:1)
37 Pierce with ox's horn (Exo. 21:29)
38 Son of Joktan (Gen. 10:26-28)
39 Moved smoothly down a surface
40 To be enclosed with a query: abbr.
41 "_____ not good for the man to be alone": 2 wds.
43 Endearing term for father: Gk.
44 Fullest extents: pl.
45 "Blood that he sprinkled on the mercy _____" (Heb. 9:7)
46 Smog
47 So be it; prayer's end (Mat. 6:13)

ACROSS

1 Ninth month in Hebrew calendar
5 What holds something closed (Joh. 1:27; KJV)
8 God "heals the ____, binding up their wounds"; woeful (Psa. 147:3)
9 Guard plotting against King Ahasuerus (Est. 2:21)
11 The Lord "isn't getting ____! He can hear you when you call" (Isa. 59:1)
15 "Praise God for ____ such loving-kindness to me"; publicly exhibiting (Ezr. 7:28)
17 Small rodent: pl. (Isa. 66:17)
19 Anyone who ____ a brother Israelite and treats him as a slave or sells him must die; carries away illegally by force (Deu. 24:7)
22 Irreverently against God or sacred things (Rev. 13:1)
24 "Who is this king of yours who ____ to plot against the Lord?" presumes (Nah. 1:11)
25 Hastened (Est. 8:14)

DOWN

1 "It is safer to meet a bear robbed of her ____ than a fool caught in his folly" (Pro. 17:12)
2 City where murderous mob stoned Paul (Act. 14:19)
3 "You must not ____"; prevaricate (Exo. 20:16)
4 Sickness (Eze. 43:25)
5 Tree's green outgrowth (Rev. 7:1)
6 To give a tenth to God (Luk. 11:42)
7 "[Wisdom] is ____ from the eyes of all mankind; even the sharp-eyed birds in the sky cannot discover it" (Job 28:17, 21)
10 "Nineveh is like a leaking water ____"; vat (Nah. 2:8)
12 "A tree is identified by the kind of fruit it produces. ____ never grow on thorns" (Luk. 6:44)
13 Esau's nickname, meaning "Red Stuff" (Gen. 25:30)
14 Knitting strands (Eze. 27:19)
16 Established as compulsory (Deu. 17:11)
18 Seat with a back (2 Ki. 4:10)
20 Large, tailless primates imported by Solomon (2 Ch. 9:21)
21 "I remained clear-____, so that I could evaluate all these things" (Ecc. 2:9)
22 "If there come any unto you, and bring not this doctrine, receive him not into your house, neither ____ him God speed"; express to (2 Jo. 1:10; KJV)
23 Solemn lyric poem (Hab. 3:19)

ACROSS

1 "The mountains melt like ____ before the Lord of all the earth"; bees' secretion (Psa. 97:5)

3 In the wrong way (Psa. 17:3)

9 Make provisions; settle details (Mk. 14:10)

11 An open sore (Lev. 13:10)

12 "God has reserved for his children the priceless gift of eternal life; it is ____ in heaven for you, pure and undefiled"; preserved (1 Pe. 1:4)

13 Oxidation of exposed metal (Hag. 2:17)

14 Drain away; gradually weaken (Hos. 5:12)

16 Distinctive individuals (Act. 18:15)

18 "A dull ____ requires great strength; be wise and sharpen the blade" (Ecc. 10:10)

20 Village where Jesus resurrected a widow's son (Luk. 7:11-14)

21 "Come, everyone, and ____ for joy! Shout triumphant praises to the Lord"; applaud (Psa. 47:1)

24 "When Christ comes back, all his people will become ____ again"; animated (1 Co. 15:23)

25 "Love forgets mistakes; ____ about them parts the best of friends"; constantly scolding (Pro. 17:9)

26 Person trained to care for others (Gen. 24:59)

27 "Jehovah keeps his ____ upon you as you come and go and always guards you"; organ of sight (Psa. 121:8)

DOWN

2 Sister of one's father or mother (Lev. 18:13)

4 "The advice of a wise man refreshes like water from a ____ spring"; elevated land higher than a hill (Pro. 13:14)

5 Bags (Gen. 44:1)

6 Strong, sudden pull (Zec. 9:7)

7 "It is senseless for you to work so hard from early morning until late at night, fearing you will starve to death; for God wants his loved ones to get their ____ rest"; suitable; right (Psa. 127:2)

8 Heavy curtains (Exo. 35:17)

10 "In this new life one's nationality or race or ____ or social position is unimportant. Whether a person has Christ is what matters"; training by formal instruction (Col. 3:11)

15 "I will bless the Lord who ____ me; he gives me wisdom in the night"; advises (Psa. 16:7)

16 Public squares or markets (Mk. 6:56)

17 Set into a surface (2 Ch. 3:6)

19 Youngest of Job's four visitors (Job 32:4)

22 What demons exorcised from two men of Gadara went into (Mk. 5:13)

23 Offensive to look at

ACROSS

1 Robe's bottom (1 Sa. 24:11)
4 Window glass
8 Small valley (Eze. 36:4)
12 Chopping tool (Deu. 19:5)
13 Son of Enoch (Gen. 4:18)
14 Judean city (Jos. 15:33, 34)
15 Samson's girlfriend (Jdg. 16:3, 4)
17 18th letter of Hebrew alphabet
18 "Straw to ____ down the camels" (Gen. 24:32)
19 Anatomy between ribs and hip (Joh. 13:4)
20 Unclothed (Gen. 2:25)
23 Asking as for charity (1 Sa. 2:36)
26 Major credit card company: abbr.
27 Speckled horse color
28 Canaanite city near Bethel (Gen. 13:3)
29 Droop
30 Long-legged wading bird (Jer. 8:7)
32 Doing business as: abbr.
33 Comparison term
34 "____ for those who persecute you!" (Mat. 5:44)
35 Edible seed pods (2 Sa. 17:28)
36 Disobedient to civil authority (Pro. 8:7)
38 Delivered; apportioned (Rut. 1:20)
39 Freedom from pain or worry (Gen. 27:39)
40 Coiling, crushing snake
41 Make a law (2 Ch. 24:6)
43 Most uncivilized (Eze. 34:25)
47 Small, sheltered bay
48 Ordered; commanded
49 Son of Noah (Gen. 5:32)
50 Employed (Gen. 47:24)
51 ____melech, Ethiopian palace official (Jer. 38:7)
52 Personal reference: Ger.

DOWN

1 Possessed (2 Ki. 8:6)
2 Last three letters of runnable computer program's name
3 Honey
4 Heaped (Jos. 4:20)
5 Country near Edom (Num. 21:2-4)
6 Expression of negation: slang
7 Process of acquiring knowledge: abbr.
8 Plan (Num. 8:4)
9 Son of Elioenai (1 Ch. 3:24)
10 Boy (Gen. 21:19)
11 Uncle: Scot.
16 Mountain goat (Deu. 14:5)
17 ____d; clad in loose Roman garment
19 ____ Patillo (Christian musician)
20 Pertaining to the nose
21 Son of Abigail (2 Sa. 17:25)
22 Small beverage barrel
23 Donkeys' cries (Job 6:5)
24 Abigail's first husband (1 Sa. 25:3)
25 Goliath, for one (1 Sa. 17:4)
30 Top of a wave
31 Carve or engrave
32 Lay minister: abbr. (Phi. 1:1)
34 Put in position (Gen. 2:8)
35 Stringed jewelry item (Sg. 4:9)
37 Make cloth (Exo. 28:39)
38 Distributed to the poor (Lev. 26:26)
40 Await; stay
41 Old French coin with shield design
42 Negatives
43 Something woven: Scot.
44 Grandson of Jacob (Gen. 46:21)
45 Strategic Air Command: abbr.
46 Tons per man hour: abbr.
48 Exist

ACROSS

1 Make a swift diving attack (Neh. 4:11)
4 Child's name meaning "there is no glory" (I Sa. 4:21)
8 Belonging to a male
9 Brother of Goliath the giant (I Ch. 20:5)
10 Sapphira's husband, killed for lying to the Lord (Act. 5:1, 3, 5)
11 Queen Esther's adoptive father (Est. 2:5, 7)
12 A temporary Canaanite home of Israel was near the Tower of ____ (Gen. 35:21)
14 Father of the 12 patriarchs of the Jewish nation (Act. 7:8)
16 Author of many musical psalms during David's reign (2 Ch. 29:30)
20 "She was the brash, coarse ____, seen often in the streets and markets, soliciting at every corner for men to be her lovers" (Pro. 7:11)
21 Criminal Pilate released instead of Jesus (Mat. 27:26)
24 O.T. author seeing vision of valley of dry bones
25 Rebecca's husband; son of Abraham (Rom. 9:10)
26 Earlier than the present (Gen. 42:8)
27 "The king appointed Shadrach, ____, and Abednego as Daniel's assistants" (Dan. 2:49)
28 "God sent those fingers to write this message: 'Mene,' 'Mene,' '____,' 'Parsin'" (Dan. 5:25)

DOWN

1 Wife of Zebedee; mother of James and John, Jesus' disciples (Mk. 15:40; Mat. 27:56)
2 Source of gold for King Solomon (I Ki. 9:28)
3 Friend of Paul; Onesimus' master
4 O.T. prophet who said, "The year King Uzziah died I saw the Lord! He was sitting on a lofty throne, and the Temple was filled with his glory"
5 "Some people like to make cutting remarks, but the words of the wise soothe and ____"; make sound or whole (Pro. 12:18)
6 Act of amassing or increasing, such as military forces: 2 wds. (I Sa. 17:2)
7 "Peter said to him, 'I will never ____ you no matter what the others do'"; abandon (Mk. 14:29)
13 Judas ____, disciple of Jesus who betrayed him (Joh. 12:4)
15 Father of Jesus' disciple Levi (Act. 2:14; NASB)
17 Steady flow of water (Deu. 9:21)
18 One of Zelophehad's five unmarried daughters (Num. 26:33)
19 Brother of Aner and Mamre, Amorite allies of Abram (Gen. 14:13)
22 Darkest color (Gen. 30:32)
23 Son of Mephibosheth; grandson of Jonathan befriended by King David (2 Sa. 9:11, 12)

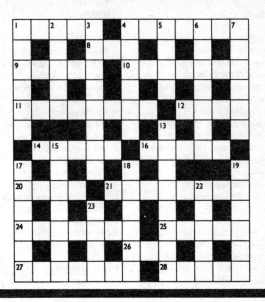

ACROSS

1 Call to mind: abbr. (Gen. 9:15)
4 Bread form (Exo. 29:23)
8 Long distance away (Isa. 30:27)
12 Wood cutter (1 Sa. 13:21)
13 Single occurrence (Gen. 29:35)
14 Narcotic
15 Repentant (Psa. 51:17)
17 Midianite general (Jdg. 7:25)
18 Combined (Gen. 30:39)
19 Short, light strokes
21 Communication standard: computer abbr.
24 Transactions (Psa. 101:3)
27 Tree wrap (Joe. 1:7)
30 Figurative name for Israel (Hos. 2:1)
32 Parts collection to assemble
33 King of Judah (1 Ki. 15:9)
34 City of Refuge (1 Ch. 6:58)
35 Rather than
36 Start of Eve (Gen. 2:22)
37 Ahira's father (Num. 1:15)
38 Judean lowland city (Jos. 15:34)
39 Abigail's husband (1 Sa. 25:3)
41 Frost
43 Same as before: Lat. abbr.
45 Son of Ishmael (Gen. 25:12, 14)
49 Water-to-wine site (Joh. 4:46)
51 Formal recording of name (Num. 3:40)
54 Idi _____ (African dictator)
55 O.T. herdsman and prophet
56 Network: abbr.
57 Tribe killing five missionaries in 1959
58 Small insects
59 "_____! Humbug!" (Scrooge)

DOWN

1 Fool: Gk.
2 Bible's second book: abbr.
3 Restore to wholeness (Gen. 6:3)
4 Dominators (Mat. 20:25)
5 "Ben_____," Rachel's dying word (Gen. 35:18)
6 Behave (Gen. 31:28)
7 Animal's nourishment (Gen. 24:32)
8 Unfired brick
9 "My God, why have you _____ me" (Mat. 27:46)
10 Chimpanzee or orangutan, e.g. (2 Ch. 9:21)
11 Addressing synagogue leader: Yid.
16 Hard, Asian wood
20 Jewish subclan head (Ezr. 2:15)
22 First murderer (Gen. 4:8)
23 Father of Micaiah, the prophet (1 Ki. 22:8)
25 Italian currency
26 Main supporting part (Exo. 37:20)
27 Animal shelter (1 Sa. 6:7)
28 _____ Minor; Turkish province (Act. 16:6; KJV)
29 Pertaining to Jewish spiritual leader (Mat. 9:18)
31 Woman's period; pref. (Lev. 12:2)
34 Joseph's father (Luk. 3:23)
38 Particular periods of history
40 River in Syria (2 Ki. 5:12)
42 Out of order (Psa. 17:3)
44 Olive brown color
46 Pierce with a knife (2 Sa. 20:10)
47 Grandson of Ham (Gen. 10:6, 7)
48 "Stone rejected has become the capstone of the _____" (Act. 4:11)
49 Credit account agreement: abbr.
50 Atomic mass unit: abbr.
52 Ostrich's relative
53 King of Meshech and Tubal (Eze. 38:2)

ACROSS

1 Swollen eyelid
5 Stringed instrument invented by Jubal (Gen. 4:21)
9 Part of Jacob's traded meal (Gen. 25:34)
12 Common; general: pref.
13 Son of Hotham (1 Ch. 7:35)
14 Computer-aided instruction: abbr.
15 Amalekite king Saul captured (1 Sa. 15:20)
16 Gifted with ability (1 Sa. 16:18)
18 Hill of _____ in southeast Jerusalem (Jer. 31:39)
20 Business agreement (2 Sa. 3:12)
21 Father: infor.
23 Prepare killed game (Pro. 12:27)
27 Samson's type of vow (Jdg. 16:17)
32 Caused sound with air (Jos. 6:16)
33 Accelerated Christian Education: abbr.
34 Make a uniform mixture
36 _____ carte: 2 wds.
37 Face covering (Job 24:15)
39 Extravagantly; costly (Isa. 46:6)
41 The way in (2 Sa. 11:13)
43 Affirmative expression
44 American Academy of Arts and Letters: abbr.
47 Second king of Israel (2 Sa. 5:3)
51 Divisions (Gen. 2:10)
55 Dreadful; urgent
56 Rowing implement (Eze. 27:6)
57 Cod relative
58 Tamar's husband (Gen. 38:8)
59 Typist's speed rating: abbr.
60 Equals three teaspoons: abbr.
61 Passed (Gen. 8:14)

DOWN

1 Heroin: slang
2 Roman garment
3 365 days (Gen. 14:4)
4 Site of David's cave hideaway (1 Sa. 23:29)
5 Head covering (1 Co. 11:4)
6 Boundary city of Asher (Jos. 19:25, 26)
7 Abnormal respiratory sound
8 Beg; implore (Exo. 8:8)
9 Fraction of whole: abbr.
10 Extended arithmetic element: abbr.
11 Help (Deu. 18:10)
17 National Labor Relations Board: abbr.
19 A sharp projection, as from the point of an arrow
22 Seasoning herb
24 King Hoshea's father (2 Ki. 15:30)
25 Exchange for money (Gen. 23:4)
26 Move back and forth (Psa. 29:9)
27 Personal designation (Gen. 12:2)
28 A round metal container: 2 wds.
29 Gusto (Eze. 23:44)
30 Leaves used for divining (Hos. 4:12)
31 Resentful awareness of another's advantage (Deu. 5:21)
35 Expired (Gen. 5:5)
38 Morton, TX radio station
40 A cast outline (2 Ki. 20:9)
42 Expensive pleasure cruise vessel
45 False prophet in Babylon (Jer. 29:20, 21)
46 Units of Albanian currency
48 "I am the true _____" (Joh. 15:1)
49 Country at war with Iraq for eight years
50 Surface depression from a blow
51 Arrow shooter (Gen. 27:3)
52 Modern poetry form?
53 Upper body limb (1 Ki. 13:6)
54 Divide: abbr. (Gen. 1:6)

	1	2	3	4		5	6	7	8		9	10	11
12						13					14		
15						16			17				
18				19		20							
		21		22			23		24	25	26		
27	28	29				30	31		32				
33				34				35		36			
37			38		39				40				
41				42			43						
		44		45	46		47		48	49	50		
51	52	53				54		55					
56				57				58					
59				60				61					

ACROSS

1 "A fool thinks he needs no ____, but a wise man listens to others" (Pro. 12:15)
5 Break in friendly relations (Gen. 13:8)
9 Having mental facilities impaired by alcohol (Gen. 9:20)
10 Understanding of the true nature of a situation (1 Co. 2:15)
11 "A relaxed ____ lengthens a man's life; jealousy rots it away"; state of mind about something (Pro. 14:30)
13 "A friendly discussion is as stimulating as the sparks that fly when ____ strikes ____" (Pro. 27:17)
15 "A man may ruin his chances by his own foolishness and then ____ it on the Lord" (Pro. 19:3)
17 "Develop good judgment and common ____" (Pro. 4:5)
21 Spoken by mouth (Dan. 1:18)
22 "God loved the world so much that he gave his only Son so that anyone who ____ in him shall not perish but have eternal life" (Joh. 3:16)
25 Verify; corroborate (Exo. 22:13)
26 Untrue; not in accordance with fact (Deu. 19:21)
27 Worthless; empty (Mat. 12:36)
28 "For he ____ down our foes" (Ps. 108:13)

DOWN

2 Be uncertain about; mistrust (Mat. 21:21)
3 Pigmented writing liquid (2 Co. 3:3)
4 Great general from tribe of Benjamin (2 Ch. 17:17)
5 Trick; deception (Gen. 27:23)
6 Calculations (Num. 26:63)
7 "The intelligent man is always open to new ____"; imaginations in the mind (Pro. 18:15)
8 "The grass withers, the flowers fade, but the Word of our God shall ____ forever"; endure (Isa. 40:8)
12 Change from wild to controllable (Jam. 3:8)
14 Another name for Matthew, tax collector turned disciple (Mk. 2:14)
16 Gained understanding by study or experience (Isa. 29:13)
18 "Be sure you know a person well before you ____ for his credit"; give a personal guarantee (Pro. 11:15)
19 "You will need the ____ of salvation and the sword of the Spirit—which is the Word of God"; mind protector (Eph. 6:17)
20 Inquired about; put a question to (Gen. 3:13)
23 "It is a badge of honor to accept ____ criticism"; founded on truth or fact (Pro. 25:12)
24 Knowing and doing the right thing (Pro. 10:8)
26 "Are you friend or ____?" enemy (Jos. 5:13)

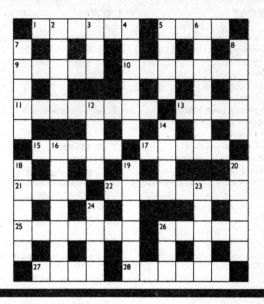

ACROSS

1 "You shall not leave in ____, running for your lives; for the Lord will go ahead of you"; rapid action (Isa. 52:12)

4 Provide care and feeding (Jer. 1:10)

8 Respond (Dan. 11:40)

9 Sudden, surprise attackers (1 Sa. 13:17)

10 "Since Christ is so much ____, the Holy Spirit warns us to listen to him"; higher or better (Heb. 3:7)

11 "Then I will ____ you of idolatry and faithlessness, and my love will know no bounds"; heal (Hos. 14:4)

13 "A true friend is always ____"; faithful (Pro. 17:17)

15 Joint between foot and leg (Act. 3:7)

19 "If the military demand that you carry their gear for a ____, carry it two"; 5280 feet (Mat. 5:41)

20 Symbolical story (Gal. 4:24; KJV)

23 "The word of God has ____ them; they don't want it at all"; aroused strong feelings of displeasure (Jer. 6:10)

24 Taut (Dan. 3:21)

25 "A beautiful woman lacking discretion and ____ is like a fine gold ring in a pig's snout"; freedom from any trace of lewdness (Pro. 11:22)

26 Series of mountains in a row (Job 39:8)

DOWN

1 "The people of Israel began once again to worship other gods, and once again the Lord let their enemies ____ them"; continually annoy (Jdg. 6:1)

2 Inundate (Luk. 8:23)

3 Relating to the outside (2 Ch. 15:6)

4 "Heaven can be entered only through the ____ gate"; less wide than normal (Mat. 7:13)

5 "One who doesn't give the gift he promised is like a cloud blowing over a desert without dropping any ____" (Pro. 25:14)

6 Without rival or similarity (Psa. 150:2)

7 "It is ____ for a camel to go through the eye of a needle than for a rich man to enter the Kingdom of God"; less difficult (Luk. 18:25)

12 Forefather (Heb. 7:9)

14 Compelled (Act. 18:14)

16 Preserve a corpse (Gen. 50:2)

17 "Anyone whose Father is God listens ____ to the words of God"; very willingly (Joh. 8:47)

18 Shiny evergreen (Zec. 1:8)

21 Bodily part performing a special function (Lev. 16:27)

22 "The magicians tried to do the same thing with their secret ____, but this time they failed"; skills (Exo. 8:18)

PUZZLE 48

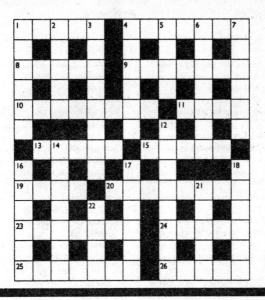

97

ACROSS

1 Cutting or tearing open (Amo. 1:13)
5 "These trials are only to see whether or not your faith is strong and pure, as fire _____ gold and purifies it"; refines or evaluates (1 Pe. 1:7)
8 "God was afraid I might be puffed up; so I was given a physical condition which has been a _____ in my flesh" (2 Co. 12:7)
9 An unbreakable stone (Zec. 7:12; KJV)
10 Next to one's sleeping space (Luk. 4:39)
12 "I, Jesus, am both David's Root and his Descendant. I am the bright Morning _____"; visible celestial body (Rev. 22:16)
16 "Swallow your pride; don't let _____ stand in the way"; self-consciousness (Pro. 6:3)
18 "I strain to reach the end of the _____ and receive the prize for which God is calling us up to heaven because of what Christ Jesus did for us"; speed contest (Phi. 3:14)
20 Is similar to (Luk. 5:36; KJV)
23 Not neat or combed
24 Cut with care, as a figure from wood (Isa. 40:20)
25 Freed from pressure or care (Psa. 73:12)
26 "Pray first that the Lord's message will spread _____ and triumph wherever it goes, winning converts everywhere"; quickly (2 Th. 3:1)

DOWN

1 First Bible book named for a woman
2 "In the mouth of a fool a _____ becomes as useless as a paralyzed leg"; maxim (Pro. 26:17)
3 Hotel (Jos. 2:1)
4 Girl born to one's child (Lev. 18:17)
5 Platter (Mat. 14:8)
6 "My children are _____ enough at doing wrong, but for doing right they have no talent"; intelligent (Jer. 4:22)
7 "Since you became alive again when Christ arose from the dead, now _____ your sights on the rich treasures and joys of heaven"; fix (Col. 3:1)
11 Waves that break on shore (Jer. 50:42)
13 Religious liturgy or ceremony (Lev. 14:19)
14 Large, heavy mammal with shaggy hair (2 Sa. 17:8)
15 Small body of land surrounded by water
17 Went into (Exo. 20:21)
19 Sweet food made from baked batter (1 Sa. 25:18)
21 Among; during
22 "If anyone wants to be a follower of mine, let him _____ himself and take up his cross and follow me": disavow (Mat. 16:24)
23 "The diligent man makes good _____ of everything he finds"; application (Pro. 12:27)
24 Head covering (Eze. 27:10)

PUZZLE 49

ACROSS

1 "Wisdom is far more valuable than gold and ____"; transparent vessel or mirror (Job 28:17)

4 Plant leaves (Eze. 19:10)

8 "That is why we never give up. Though our bodies are dying, our ____ strength in the Lord is growing every day"; opposite of outer (2 Co. 4:16)

9 "Of all the beasts, [the crocodile] is the proudest—____ of all that he sees"; sovereign (Job 41:1, 34)

10 "A good reputation is more ____ than the most expensive perfume"; of great importance (Ecc. 7:1)

11 "What is wrong cannot be righted; it is water ____ the dam; and there is no use thinking of what might have been"; past (Ecc. 1:15)

13 Small containers, usually enclosed (Mk. 12:41)

15 "As all the people watched, Solomon ____ down, reached out his arms toward heaven, and prayed this prayer" (2 Ch. 6:13)

19 Beat with a whip (Act. 22:25)

20 Estrange (Eze. 48:14; KJV)

23 "Your throne, O God, endures forever. Justice is your royal ____"; staff signifying authority (Psa. 45:6)

24 Gradually diminished (2 Co. 3:11)

DOWN

1 Feel sorrow for (Rut. 1:13)

2 Render void (Eph. 2:15)

3 "I ____, 'I'm slipping, Lord!' and he was kind and saved me"; cried loudly" (Psa. 94:18)

4 "The fool who provokes his ____ to anger and resentment will finally have nothing worthwhile left"; parents and children (Pro. 11:29)

5 "There will always be some among you who are poor. You must ____ to them liberally"; give temporarily (Deu. 15:11)

6 "Everyone must straighten out his life to be ready for the Lord's ____"; coming (Mk. 1:3)

7 "I ____ you to be of good cheer"; urge earnestly (Act. 27:22; KJV)

12 Jesus said, "The world's sin is ____ in me"; lack of trust (Joh. 16:9)

14 Make dim or partly hidden (Hab. 3:11)

16 Solid pieces of a hard substance with flat sides (1 Ki. 5:17)

17 Musician (1 Sa. 16:18)

18 Cut down (2 Ki. 3:25)

21 "A sensible man watches for problems ____ and prepares to meet them"; in the future (Pro. 27:12)

22 "Those who still reject me are like the restless sea, which is never still, but always churns up mire and ____"; soil (Isa. 57:20)

PUZZLE 50

ACROSS

1 People of country bordering Egypt (2 Ch. 16:8)
5 "The whole land is full of images, and the people are _____ in love with their idols"; wildly (Jer. 50:38)
8 "Jehoiada the priest bored a hole in the lid of a large chest . . . and the doorkeepers put all of the people's _____ into it" (2 Ki. 12:9)
9 "I want those already wise to become the wiser and become leaders by exploring the depths of meaning in these _____ of truth"; lumps of gold (Pro. 1:5)
11 God "_____ swiftly to my aid with wings of wind" (Psa. 18:10)
15 Involuntarily (Num. 30:5)
17 "The priceless gift of eternal life . . . is _____ in heaven for you, pure and undefiled, beyond the reach of change and decay"; preserved (1 Pe. 1:4)
19 Urban thoroughfares (Est. 6:11)
22 "Not using your liberty for a cloke of _____, but as the servants of God"; ill will (1 Pe. 2:16; KJV)
24 Disciple who walked on water (Mat. 14:29)
25 "We—every one of us—have _____ away like sheep"; wandered (Isa. 53:6)

DOWN

1 Stroke the tongue over (Eze. 23:34)
2 "Let us be glad and rejoice and honor him; for the time has come for the wedding _____ of the Lamb"; ceremonial dinner (Rev. 19:7)
3 What Absalom dangled in by his hair (2 Sa. 18:9)
4 Replacements (Lev. 27:33)
5 Partner (Isa. 34:16)
6 "My health fails; my spirits _____, yet God remains! He is the strength of my heart"; sag (Psa. 73:26)
7 Expression of consent (Gen. 3:12)
10 "A lazy man won't even dress the _____ he gets while hunting" (Pro. 12:27)
12 "Our _____ here on earth are as transient as shadows"; 24-hour periods (Job 8:9)
13 "Let not the wise man _____ in his wisdom"; revel (Jer. 9:23)
14 "Our hearts _____, but at the same time we have the joy of the Lord" (2 Co. 6:10)
16 Drawing for prizes (Jos. 19:51)
18 "A tiny rudder makes a huge ship turn wherever the _____ wants it to go"; helmsman (Jam. 3:4)
20 Lingering sign of damage (Gal. 6:17)
21 Employed (Exo. 3:15)
22 Travel guide (Eze. 4:1)
23 Respectful address to a man (Gen. 24:18)

PUZZLE 51

ACROSS

1 Violent outburst (Act. 19:23)
5 "My _____ to you is this: Go to God and confess your sins to him"; suggestion (Job 5:8)
8 "Rest in the Lord; wait patiently for him to _____"; produce an effect (Psa. 37:7)
9 "A wise man is mightier than a _____ man"; physically powerful (Pro. 24:5)
10 "God _____ displayed to the whole world Christ's triumph at the cross where your sins were all taken away"; publicly (Col. 2:15)
11 "It is wrong to sentence the poor and let the rich go _____"; at liberty (Pro. 24:23)
12 "The king appointed Shadrach, Meshach, and _____ as Daniel's assistants" (Dan. 2:49)
14 "To me, living means _____ for Christ"; favorable times (Phi. 1:21)
17 "I have _____ against thee, because thou hast left thy first love"; rather; to a certain degree (Rev. 2:4; KJV)
19 Affected, artificial manners (2 Co. 11:20)
21 Performer (1 Sa. 16:18)
23 Divine revelation (Exo. 28:15)
24 Word meaning "son" in Hebrew (Amo. 1:4)
25 Affairs or points of controversy (Jdg. 9:35)
26 Regular wage for work done (1 Co. 9:19)

DOWN

2 "Give generously, for your gifts will return to you _____"; at a subsequent time (Ecc. 11:1)
3 "Let us purify ourselves, living in the _____ fear of God, giving ourselves to him alone"; conducive to spiritual health (2 Co. 7:1)
4 Elaborate procession (Rev. 15:1)
5 Make satisfaction or payment for (Lev. 4:28)
6 Contend (2 Ch. 35:18)
7 "Wear fine clothes—with a dash of _____"; perfumed liquid (Ecc. 9:8)
13 Disciple to whom Jesus said, "I could see you under the fig tree before Philip found you" (Joh. 1:48)
15 "You shall be holy to me, for I the Lord am holy, and I have set you apart from all other _____ to be mine"; races (Lev. 20:26)
16 "The glory and honor of all the _____ shall be brought into the city of God"; political entities (Rev. 21:26)
18 Plants used for seasoning or medicine (Mk. 15:23)
20 "Christ is the highest _____, with authority over every other power"; political figure (Col. 2:10)
22 "_____ are the world's seasoning, to make it tolerable"; direct address (Mat. 5:13)

ACROSS

1 Judge or faultfinder (Job 40:2)
5 Deprived of something (Jer. 18:21)
8 Son of Abdiel (1 Ch. 5:15)
9 Young woman (Gen. 24:16; KJV)
10 "When you give a gift to a ____, don't shout about it as the hypocrites do"; panhandler (Mat. 6:2)
11 "Take off your ____, for you are standing on holy ground"; foot covering: sing. (Exo. 3:5)
12 One's name and personal recognition factors (Act. 7:13)
14 "I pray to the Father that out of his glorious, unlimited resources he will give you the mighty inner ____ of his Holy Spirit"; making healthier (Eph. 3:16)
18 "When darkness overtakes the man who delights in doing God's commands, light will come ____ in"; suddenly breaking out (Psa. 112:4)
20 "Go ____ on others; then they will do the same for you"; not hard (Luk. 6:37)
22 Cling to (Act. 15:1)
24 "If a soul commit a trespass, and sin through ignorance, he shall make ____ for the harm that he hath done"; reparations (Lev. 5:15, 16; KJV)
25 Damage; jeopardize (Rut. 4:6; KJV)
26 "Release all the animals, birds, and reptiles, so that they will ____ abundantly and reproduce in great numbers"; propagate (Gen. 8:17)
27 "Do not bring an idol into your home and worship it, for then your doom is sealed. Utterly ____ it, for it is a cursed thing"; hate (Deu. 7:26)

DOWN

2 "Eternal peace was within your ____ and you turned it down"; grasp (Luk. 19:42)
3 "Even honey seems ____ to a man who is full; but if he is hungry, he'll eat anything"; without flavor (Pro. 27:7)
4 Making watertight (Eze. 27:9)
5 "A pastor must enjoy having guests in his home and must be a good ____ teacher"; Scripture (1 Ti. 3:2)
6 Soft floor covering (Lev. 11:32)
7 "No mountain, however high, can stand before Zerubbabel! For it will ____ out before him"; make smooth (Zec. 4:7)
11 Female sibling: inform. (Gen. 19:31)
13 Softest; most chewable (Amo. 6:4)
15 "The mighty oceans ____ your praise"; sound following lightning (Psa. 93:3)
16 Worn or emaciated (2 Sa. 13:4)
17 Happy; lighthearted
19 Thing in a series or collection (Num. 3:31)
21 Front and back, as of a scroll (Eze. 2:10)
23 Until (Hos. 8:5; KJV)

ACROSS

1 "Stand before the Lord in ____, and do not sin against him"; reverential wonder (Psa. 4:4)
3 Walking (Mk. 6:33; KJV)
9 Gathers; accumulates (1 Ch. 29:25)
11 Become liable for
12 Dry and barren
13 Sign or warning for the future (Luk. 21:25)
14 Male sheep (Mal. 1:14)
16 "Adam's sin brought punishment to all, but Christ's ____ makes men right with God, so that they can live"; moral excellence (Rom. 5:18)
18 Edge of a curved object (2 Ch. 4:2)
20 Turn an animal by a bridle part (2 Ki. 9:23)
21 "In our greatness we have gathered up kingdoms as a farmer gathers ____"; hard-shelled reproductive bodies (Isa. 10:14)
24 Mountain where Moses received the Ten Commandments (Exo. 31:18)
25 "Some astrologers arrived in Jerusalem, asking, 'Where is the newborn King of the Jews? for we have seen his star in far-off ____ lands and have come to worship him'"; direction (Mat. 2:1, 2)
26 Light-colored silicate mineral (Rev. 21:20)
27 Body of water nearly surrounded by land (Jos. 15:2)

DOWN

2 "____ me and I shall be whiter than snow"; cleanse as with a liquid (Psa. 51:7)
4 "God will judge them with complete ____, for all heaven declares that he is just" (Psa. 50:6)
5 "This book unveils some of the future activities soon to ____ in the life of Jesus Christ"; take place (Rev. 1:1)
6 "This miracle at ____ in Galilee was Jesus' first public demonstration of his heaven-sent power. And his disciples believed that he really was the Messiah" (Joh. 2:11)
7 Cooking by dry heat (1 Ki. 19:6)
8 "Even the puppies beneath the table are permitted to eat the ____ that fall"; small fragments (Mat. 15:27)
10 Serve as the counterpart or image of (Eze. 21:14)
15 "God has planted ____ in the hearts of men"; unending duration (Ecc. 3:11)
16 Most extraordinary; least seen (Sg. 6:1)
17 Large birds of prey (Hab. 1:8)
19 Walk in a prim, affected manner (Isa. 3:16)
22 "A rebel's frustrations are heavier than ____ and rocks"; loose, granular rock particles (Pro. 27:3)
23 "Epaenetus was the very first person to become a Christian in ____"; Roman region northwest of Syria (Rom. 16:5)

ACROSS

1 Cherished animal companions (2 Sa. 12:3)
5 Biographer of Solomon; O.T. prophet (2 Ch. 9:29)
9 Directly across from: abbr. (Num. 34:14)
12 Beginning; end; extremity: pref.
13 Mustard or God's message, e.g. (Luk. 8:11; 13:19)
14 Father of Abner, King Saul's general (1 Sa. 14:51)
15 Brilliantly executed strategem
16 Survived fiery furnace (Dan. 3:23-25)
18 Aaron's son (Exo. 6:23)
20 Ship's distress signal
21 Unspoken; implied
23 Faint streak
26 Type of computer printer
29 Sarai's relation to Abram: infor.
31 _____ culpa
32 Conspirator (Num. 16:1, 2)
34 Prophet to Saul and David (1 Sa. 10:1; 19:18)
36 Last O.T. book: abbr.
37 Female domestic fowl (Luk. 13:34)
39 Assigned work (1 Ch. 6:49)
40 Public notice: abbr.
42 King Jeroboam's father (1 Ki. 11:26)
44 Eighth month: abbr. (Ezr. 7:9)
46 _____ Pilate (Act. 4:27)
50 Woman who quarreled with Euodias (Phi. 4:2)
53 "Quota _____ est?": Lat.
54 Promissory note
55 Look intently into (Luk. 24:12)
56 Female sheep: pl. (Gen. 30:40)
57 Long passenger carrier
58 Sharp-toothed tools (2 Sa. 12:31)
59 Habits; characteristics (Gen. 6:3)

DOWN

1 Walking step (Gen. 33:14)
2 Related to environment: abbr.
3 Consistent with reality (Gen. 45:28)
4 Paul's traveling companion (Act. 20:4)
5 Son nearly sacrificed by Abraham (Gen. 22:2)
6 Scattered remains (Act. 27:44)
7 Fourth letter
8 Probabalities (Jdg. 5:13)
9 Converted runaway slave (Phm. 1:10)
10 Cylindrical fastener (Jdg. 4:21)
11 Expert (Act. 4:13)
17 At present time (Gen. 2:25)
19 Son of Judah and Tamar (Gen. 38:30; KJV)
22 "_____ the season to be jolly"
24 Search for (1 Ch. 16:11)
25 Chums: infor.
26 "Eli, Eli, _____ sabachthani" (Mat. 27:46)
27 "Won't risk having _____ conscience: 2 wds. (1 Co. 10:27)
28 Paul's co-worker (2 Co. 1:19)
30 Job's accuser (Job 1:6)
33 Adult males (Gen. 10:32)
35 Tax collector turned disciple
38 Lot's relation to Abraham (Gen. 12:4, 5)
41 Egyptian King _____'s treasures
43 South Africans of Dutch descent
45 Swindle; defraud
47 Central U.S. state
48 Am. chemist, Harold Clayton _____
49 Impertinence; back talk
50 Blood relation
51 "What profit is there if _____ gain the whole world" (Mat. 16:26)
52 Council of Economic Advisors: abbr.

ACROSS

1 Polished, precious stone (Rev. 21:11)
4 Every (Gen. 6:20)
8 King of Amalekites (1 Sa. 15:8)
12 Physicians' organization: abbr.
13 Liver liquid
14 Summoned
15 Moses' wife (Exo. 2:21)
17 Father of Zechariah (Ezr. 5:1)
18 Intentionally-set fire
19 Sea east of Judah (2 Ki. 14:25)
21 Affirmative oral vote
23 Customary behavior (Rom. 12:13)
27 Sharp part of a plow (1 Sa. 13:21)
30 City of David; Jerusalem (2 Sa. 5:7)
33 Beer-like beverage
34 One of Lamech's wives (Gen. 4:19)
35 Complete; stop (Exo. 9:28)
36 Group of relatives (Gen. 36:17)
37 Normal; customary: abbr. (Exo. 5:18)
38 Passed-on practice: abbr. (Joh. 7:22)
39 Flower garlands
40 King David's choir leader (Neh. 12:46)
42 Small Business Administration: abbr.
44 Piece of tree foliage (Gen. 8:11)
47 Prevaricators (Psa. 12:3)
51 Son of King Rehoboam (2 Ch. 11:18-20)
54 Jewish governor; returned exile
56 Single facial spasm: 2 wds.
57 Related to Confucians' beliefs
58 Acute care admission: abbr.
59 Open wide, as jaws (Job 16:10)
60 Make a long, narrow cut (1 Sa. 24:4)
61 Once owned

DOWN

1 Strip of land in western Israel (Gen. 10:19)
2 Arabian governor
3 Journey guides (Psa. 119:19)
4 Dark, valuable wood (Eze. 27:15)
5 Atmosphere (Psa. 140:5)
6 Clothed
7 Foolish giggle
8 Son of Midian (Gen. 25:4)
9 Hebrew tribe (Num. 34:14)
10 Augment (Deu. 4:2)
11 Related to the earth: pref. (Gen. 10:31)
16 Take game by trespassing
20 Army health nurse: abbr.
22 Jewish cattle rustler (1 Ch. 7:21)
24 Bundled hay
25 Famous warrior (1 Ch. 11:26, 29)
26 Groups of 10 (Exo. 18:25)
27 Son of Zerah (1 Ch. 2:6)
28 Middle of month in ancient Roman calendar
29 Long, heroic narrative
31 "Like peas ____ pod": 2 wds.
32 Probabilities; chances (Jdg. 5:13)
36 Legal right to a settlement (Gen. 20:16)
38 Particularization pronoun (Gen. 1:1)
41 Specific location (Gen. 2:21)
43 Generations "forever shall call me ____ of God" (Luk. 1:48)
45 Diligent insects (Pro. 6:6)
46 Faithful; loyal: arch.
48 Rizpah's father (2 Sa. 21:8)
49 ____ l; city (1 Sa. 30:27, 29)
50 Fish spawning upstream
51 Counterpart to zig
52 Lighter, slanted type: abbr.
53 Fast, energetic movement
55 ____ poloi

ACROSS

1 "No one can ____ them from me"; carry away by force (Joh. 10:29)
5 "To enjoy your work and to ____ your lot in life—that is indeed a gift from God" (Ecc. 5:20)
8 "We toss the coin, but it is the Lord who controls ____ decision" (Pro. 16:33)
9 Nullify (Isa. 28:18)
10 Set on fire (Job 41:21)
11 Gave a new color to (Exo. 36:19)
12 "Because of this ____ upon Moses' face, Aaron and the people of Israel were afraid" (Exo. 34:30)
14 "This is the day ____ the atonement, cleansing you in the Lord's eyes"; celebrating (Lev. 16:30)
17 "I will reestablish the land of Israel and ____ it to its own people again"; allot again (Isa. 49:8)
19 "If the boss is angry with you, don't ____! A quiet spirit will quiet his bad temper"; resign (Ecc. 10:4)
21 One of Hazzelponi's brothers (1 Ch. 4:3)
23 "We are always confident, knowing that, ____ we are at home in the body, we are absent from the Lord"; at the time of (2 Co. 5:6; KJV)
24 Abijam's son; king of Judah (1 Ki. 15:7, 8)
25 Temporary indirect route (Isa. 33:8)
26 Nonmembers of the religious clergy (2 Ch. 11:16)

DOWN

2 Original country of Aquila and Priscilla (Act. 18:2)
3 Jewish leader to whom Jesus said, "Unless you are born again, you can never get into the Kingdom of God" (Joh. 3:3, 4)
4 "I am but a ____ here on earth: how I need a map—and your commands are my chart and guide"; traveler (Psa. 119:19)
5 "This is what I have ____ of God for you: that you will be encouraged"; requested (Col. 2:2)
6 "I ____ do everything God asks me to with the help of Christ" (Phi. 4:13)
7 Large-billed sea bird (Deu. 14:17)
13 Ancient age (Isa. 23:7; KJV)
15 Late (Hab. 2:3)
16 A beginning again; restoration (2 Ch. 16:3)
18 A son of King David (1 Ch. 3:6)
20 "Without making a big ____ over it, God simply shatters the greatest of men and puts others in their places"; point of controversy (Job 34:24)
22 Prior (Deu. 1:6)

PUZZLE 57

ACROSS

1 "I saw a great white throne and the one who ____ upon it" (Rev. 20:11)
4 Group of families (Gen. 19:32)
8 Boast (Amo. 4:5)
12 Finnish seaport
13 Turkish or Syrian pound
14 Possess (Phi. 4:18)
15 Largest computer company: abbr.
16 Grandson of Noah (Gen. 10:21)
17 Twelfth month of Hebrew year (Est. 3:7; KJV)
18 Hard work (Jer. 22:13)
20 Assert positively
22 Years attained (Gen. 5:5)
24 "They shall mount up with wings like ____" (Isa. 40:31)
28 Ones killed for their faith (Rev. 14:13)
32 To blind or close eyes to: arch.
33 Intensive care unit: abbr.
34 Help or support (Rom. 15:27)
36 Pen point
37 "He is like a blazing fire refining precious ____" (Mal. 3:2)
40 ____ Ghandi
43 Valley (Num. 13:23)
45 Open: arch.
46 Black, solid fuel (Isa. 6:6)
48 Kingdom (2 Ch. 32:22)
52 Jesus "will ____ his people"
55 Appearance guarantee money (Act. 17:8)
57 Denial; no
58 As soon as possible: abbr.
59 4,840 sq. yds. of land (Isa. 5:10)
60 Yearly recurrence: abbr. (Deu. 16:6)
61 Small, arrowlike missile (Job 41:26)
62 Something required (Exo. 25:39)
63 New Zealand parrot

DOWN

1 Travel on wind (1 Ki. 9:28)
2 Father: Gk.
3 Where Jesus' body placed (Joh. 19:42)
4 Ordained ministerial order (1 Sa. 22:17)
5 Book collection: abr. (Ezr. 5:17)
6 Open space (Num. 3:38)
7 Courage (1 Sa. 13:6)
8 Command (Gen. 41:42)
9 Energy unit
10 Eggs
11 Who: Ger.
19 Edible cereal grass seed
21 Eastern Airlines System: abbr.
23 Period of history
25 Ash Wednesday to Easter
26 Wilderness oasis Hebrews visited (Num. 33:9)
27 Region of Ethiopia (Isa. 43:3)
28 Portray silently
29 Gets the better of: slang
30 King David's great-grandmother (Mat. 1:5, 6)
31 Sudan Interior Mission: abbr.
35 Father: infor.
38 "Be a living sacrifice, holy—the kind he can ____" (Rom. 12:1)
39 Old card game
41 Throw forcefully (1 Sa. 17:49)
42 Large primate (1 Ki. 10:22)
44 Jacob's father-in-law (Gen. 29:23)
47 Delicate, open fabric
49 Father of three giants (Jos. 15:14)
50 Narrow road (Luk. 14:23)
51 Asian starling
52 Unhappy; unfortunate (1 Ki. 14:6)
53 Judean king
54 Change; alter: abbr.
56 Anger

PUZZLE 58

117

ACROSS

1 Driven or thrown out (Jer. 52:3)
5 Device for holding things together (Exo. 36:13)
8 "Your ____ is caused by your ignorance of the Scriptures and of God's power"; mistake (Mat. 22:29)
9 "Come, all of you who are skilled craftsmen having special ____, and construct what God has commanded us"; abilities (Exo. 35:10)
10 Rooms below ground level (1 Ch. 27:28; KJV)
12 Adult castrated bulls (Psa. 144:14)
16 "David prayed, 'O Lord God, why have you showered your blessings on such an ____ person as I am?'"; unimportant (2 Sa. 7:18)
18 "Don't ____ evil men but continue to reverence the Lord all the time, for surely you have a wonderful future ahead of you"; resentful awareness of another's advantage (Pro. 23:17)
20 Something purchased for less than its value (Pro. 20:14)
23 Member of Hebrew race (Exo. 5:14)
24 "____ his courts with praise. Give thanks to him and bless his name"; go in (Psa. 100:4)
25 Bloodsucking worm (Pro. 30:15)
26 "God took this list of sins and destroyed it by ____ it to Christ's cross"; fastening with metal spikes (Col. 2:14)

DOWN

1 Adam and Eve's home (Gen. 2:8)
2 Those receiving wages or profit for their efforts (Gen. 30:26)
3 Sealing liquid distilled from coal (Gen. 6:14)
4 Firm purpose (Act. 3:13)
5 Shape of golden idol the Hebrews made at Mount Sinai (Exo. 32:8)
6 Added-on building (1 Ki. 6:5)
7 Yellowish fluid forming in an infected sore (Job 7:5)
11 Trees cut for lumber (Ezr. 3:7)
13 "If you endorse a ____ for someone you hardly know, guaranteeing his debt, you are in serious trouble"; written promise to pay (Pro. 6:1)
14 "The man who finds a ____ finds a good thing; she is a blessing to him from the Lord"; marriage partner (Pro. 18:22)
15 Male monarch (Gen. 12:15)
17 Father of the prophet Jonah (2 Ki. 14:25)
19 "How constantly I find myself upon the ____ of sin; this source of sorrow always stares me in the face"; threshold (Psa. 38:17)
21 Rachel's older sister; Jacob's first wife (Gen. 29:16, 23)
22 "Don't ____ about your plans for tomorrow—wait and see what happens"; talk boastfully (Pro. 27:1)
23 Sick (Joh. 5:6)
24 Samuel's priestly mentor and guardian (1 Sa. 2:11)

PUZZLE 59

ACROSS

1 "Even the _____ of them, though they have hearts of lions, will be paralyzed with fear"; most courageous (2 Sa. 17:10)

5 The region of seven churches to which John wrote (1 Co. 16:19)

8 "He _____ the little pet lamb in his arms like a baby daughter"; held close (2 Sa. 12:3)

9 "When there is _____ rot within a nation, its government topples easily"; according to basic principles of right (Pro. 28:2)

10 "Evil men have tried to _____ me into sin, but I am firmly anchored to your laws"; pull (Psa. 119:61)

11 Providers of money for temporary use (Isa. 24:2)

13 Mutual associations (Rom. 1:27)

15 "A man should only make a vow he _____ to keep" (Deu. 5:11)

17 "Jerusalem's streets _____ with the sounds of violence"; reflect sound (Jer. 6:7)

20 "Rich and poor are _____ in this: each depends on God for light"; similar (Pro. 29:13)

21 "How _____ are thy tabernacles, O LORD of hosts"; easy to get along with (Psa. 84:1; KJV)

22 "Where is the man who fears the Lord? God will teach him how to choose the _____"; most excellent (Psa. 25:12)

23 Pull taut (1 Ch. 18:3)

DOWN

1 "A rebuke to a man of common sense is more effective than a hundred lashes on the _____ of a rebel"; part nearest the spine (Pro. 17:10)

2 "In the end strong wine bites like a poisonous serpent; it stings like an _____" (Pro. 23:32)

3 "Daniel, I have heard that you have the spirit of the gods within you and that you are filled with _____ and wisdom"; spiritual insight (Dan. 5:14)

4 King of Goiim (Gen. 14:1)

5 "'We should spend our time preaching, not _____ a feeding program,' the Twelve said"; managing (Act. 6:2)

6 Member of the Hebrew nation (Exo. 9:6)

7 Most intimate (Joh. 13:23)

12 "Proclaim that everyone must straighten out his life to be ready for the Lord's _____"; coming (Mk. 1:3)

14 Framework of crossed strips (1 Ki. 7:21)

16 Barely sufficient (Hag. 1:10)

18 "Get into the _____ of inviting guests home for dinner or, if they need lodging, for the night"; usual practice (Rom. 12:13)

19 Mentally alert; acute (Jer. 13:27)

ACROSS

1 Type of large boat Noah built (Gen. 8:18)
3 "Wisdom is better than weapons of war, but one rotten ____ can spoil a barrelful"; round, firm fruit with white flesh (Ecc. 9:18)
9 Work out by mutual agreement (Mk. 14:10)
11 Make amends or satisfaction for (Lev. 4:28)
12 Bottom (Exo. 19:2)
13 "So that Christ could give her to himself as a glorious Church without a single ____ or wrinkle or any other blemish" (Eph. 5:27)
14 Second book of the Bible: abbr.
16 "Who else is like the Lord among the gods? Who is glorious in holiness like him? Who is so awesome in splendor, A ____ God?"; miracle-doing (Exo. 15:11)
18 Wane; decrease in strength (Deu. 32:36)
20 "Meanwhile little Samuel was helping the Lord by assisting Eli. Messages from the Lord were very ____ in those days"; infrequent (1 Sa. 3:1)
21 Affected, artificial manner (2 Co. 11:20)
24 Transported goods (Jon. 1:5)
25 Reduced to a lower rank (1 Sa. 18:13)
26 Deadly pale (Jer. 30:6)
27 "You are a letter from Christ, written by us. It is not a letter written with pen and ____, but by the Spirit of the living God; not one carved on stone, but in human hearts" (2 Co. 3:3)

DOWN

2 "Again and again their voices ____, 'Praise the Lord!'"; resounded (Rev. 19:3)
4 Ancient musical instrument similar to a zither (1 Sa. 10:5)
5 "Let ____ your lightning bolts, your arrows, Lord, upon your enemies, and scatter them"; unrestrained (Psa. 144:6)
6 Clothing (2 Ki. 25:29)
7 Returned from the dead (Col. 1:18)
8 "If you ____ to the Lord, reverence him; for everyone who does this has everything he needs"; are related to (Psa. 34:9)
10 "If I am ____ by Satan, what about your own followers? For they cast out demons"; authorized by (Luk. 11:19)
15 Terror-causing (Psa. 22:12)
16 Miserable, unhappy, vile person (Mat. 18:32)
17 Feeble-minded or foolish persons (Joh. 11:49)
19 "Honor the Lord by giving him the first part of all your income, and he will fill your ____ with wheat and barley"; farm buildings (Pro. 3:9)
22 "Any story sounds true until someone tells the other ____ and sets the record straight" (Pro. 18:17)
23 "Don't bring us into temptation, but deliver us from the Evil One. ____" (Mat. 6:13)

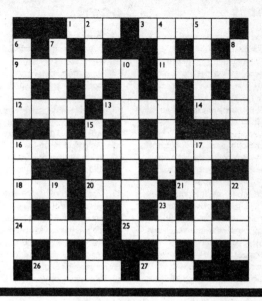

ACROSS

1 Mold for pouring metal (Exo. 38:30)
5 "As newborn ____, desire the sincere milk of the word, that ye may grow thereby" (1 Pe. 2:2; KJV)
8 Put identification slip on (Jer. 6:30)
9 "The Lord your God is merciful—he will not ____ you nor destroy you nor forget the promises he has made to your ancestors"; desert (Deu. 4:31)
10 Oval, edible nuts with soft, light-brown shell (Num. 17:8)
12 "The bird returned to him with an olive leaf in her ____. So Noah knew that the water was almost gone" (Gen. 8:11)
16 "Because of God's deep love and concern for you, you should practice ____ mercy and kindness to others"; compassionate (Col. 3:12)
18 Postal service deliveries (Est. 8:14)
20 Frightened (Dan. 1:10)
23 Pillow or support (1 Sa. 26:16; KJV)
24 The devil (Rev. 12:9)
25 "It is ____ to make loans to strangers"; liability to loss (Pro. 20:16)
26 Closest (Gen. 28:19)

DOWN

1 Young cow (Gen. 18:7)
2 Extended family or tribal division (Num. 26:29)
3 "____gotten gain brings no lasting happiness; right living does"; wrongly (Pro. 10:2)
4 "An old man's ____ are his crowning glory"; offspring of one's son or daughter (Pro. 17:6)
5 The god of Moab (Num. 25:3)
6 "It is a ____ of honor to accept valid criticism"; symbol of status (Pro. 25:12)
7 "The wages of ____ is death, but the free gift of God is eternal life through Jesus Christ our Lord"; offense against God (Rom. 6:23)
11 "Evil men borrow and 'cannot pay it back'! But the good man returns what he ____ with some extra besides" (Ps. 37:21)
13 Young goats (Isa. 5:17)
14 "All the other commandments and all the demands of the prophets ____ from these two laws"; flow (Mat. 22:40)
15 Threadlike growths from skin (Gen. 25:25)
17 Auditorium (Act. 19:29; KJV)
19 "Hard work means prosperity; only a fool ____ away his time"; does nothing (Pro. 12:11)
21 "____ true to what is right and God will bless you and use you to help others"; remain (1 Ti. 4:16)
22 "Blind guides! You strain out a ____ and swallow a camel"; small, biting fly (Mat. 23:24)
23 Long, narrow strip of wood (Exo. 36:23)
24 Large body of salt water (Gen. 49:13)

ACROSS

1 Oval fowl foods (Job 39:14)
5 Walk through impeding substance
9 Male sibling: abbr. (Gen. 4:2)
12 Public uproar (Act. 17:5)
13 Boat steering devices (Eze. 27:6)
14 Army air base: abbr.
15 Prophetess Anna's tribe (Luk. 2:36; KJV)
16 Lifting up: pl. (Eze. 26:8)
18 Inflicted a blow (Gen. 32:25)
20 "In the day that thou ____ thereof thou shalt surely die" (Gen. 2:17; KJV)
21 Type of hat
22 Color changer (Eze. 27:7)
23 Festival of Tabernacles month: abbr.
26 Resting place (1 Sa. 3:2)
28 Comparatively little (Gen. 19:20)
32 Leading citizen of Shechem (Jdg. 9:26)
34 Basketball league: abbr.
36 Wound's crust (Lev. 14:56)
37 Spirited mount (Zec. 10:3)
39 Son of Benjamin (Gen. 46:21)
41 Major network: abbr.
42 Fair equivalent: abbr. (Exo. 22:4)
44 Defendant: var.
46 Tranquil (Isa. 18:4)
49 Changes (Ezr. 6:12)
53 Subject of seventh commandment (Exo. 20:14)
55 "____ every law of your government" (1 Pet. 2:13)
56 Nott and ____ (gods)
57 O.T. book after Proverbs: abbr.
58 Town where Jesus brought a boy back to life (Luk. 7:11-14)
59 Physicians' professional organization: abbr.
60 Food fish
61 Other; in addition (Exo. 20:17)

DOWN

1 Distinguishable periods of time
2 Central idea
3 One who proceeds
4 Walk pompously (Psa. 73:9)
5 Skilled manual laborers (Exo. 28:5)
6 Chicago Motor Club, e.g.: abbr.
7 What God did to Red Sea and Jordan River (Jos. 4:23)
8 Short compositions on a theme
9 Cause of death or ruin
10 Worn-out scraps of cloth (Lam. 1:17)
11 Headstrong: abbr. (Isa. 48:4)
17 Specific parts of a collection (Exo. 29:33)
19 Taxi
23 "We turned toward King ____ land of Bashan" (Deu. 3:1)
24 Catches rats and mice
25 Take: Scot.
27 Sole proprietorship alias designation: abbr.
29 American Academy of arts: abbr.
30 Scientific experimentation site: infor.
31 Units of weight = 16 oz.: abbr.
33 Flat; horizontal (Luk. 6:17)
35 Arranged in order (Job 6:4)
38 Belonging to author of The Inferno
40 Computer command to erase a file
43 Blood sucker (Pro. 30:15)
45 Make amends for; cover (Lev. 4:28)
46 Seismic array data analyzer: abbr.
47 Experiment, drill, and maintainence: mil. abbr.
48 Visceral wrinkle
50 Son of Shobal (Gen. 36:23)
51 Belonging to a loyalist of King David (1 Ki. 1:8)
52 Since then: Scot.
54 NYC music hall

PUZZLE 63

1
2
3
4
5
6
7
8
9
10
11
12
13
14
15
16
17
18
19
20
21
22
23
24
25
26
27
28
29
30
31
32
33
34
35
36
37
38
39
40
41
42
43
44
45
46
47
48
49
50
51
52
53
54
55
56
57
58
59
60
61

ACROSS

1 "Let God _____ you, for he is doing what any loving father does for his children"; cause to grow as desired (Heb. 12:7)

4 Vertical sections of a printed page (Jer. 36:23)

8 "Some men enjoy cheating, but the cake they buy with such _____-gotten gain will turn to gravel in their mouths" (Pro. 20:17)

9 Paul had one of these in his flesh to keep him humble (2 Co. 12:7)

10 An ephah equals about _____ bushel of dry measure: 2 wds. (Eze. 45:11)

11 Number of men who died when the Tower of Siloam fell on them (Luk. 13:4)

12 Sixth month (Ezr. 3:8)

14 King Solomon "had seven hundred _____ ... and they turned his heart away from the Lord" (1 Ki. 11:3)

16 "When a good man speaks, he is worth listening to, but the words of fools are a dime a _____" (Pro. 10:20)

20 "A lazy fellow has trouble all through life; the good man's path is _____"; not hard (Pro. 15:19)

21 "The _____ year shall be holy, a time to proclaim liberty throughout the land" (Lev. 25:10)

24 Large, level area raised above its surroundings (Num. 21:20)

25 Enthusiastic; anxious (2 Ch. 26:5)

26 Make delicate handmade lace

27 At farthest point; end of a range (Eze. 46:19)

28 Angrily

DOWN

1 "Bring all the _____ into the storehouse"; tenths (Mal. 3:10)

2 In the number of (Gen. 7:1)

3 Number of cities given Hebrew tribe of Naphtali (Jos. 19:32, 39)

4 Divided into two; split (Lev. 11:7)

5 "_____ will get any man into trouble, but honesty is its own defense" (Pro. 12:13)

6 "Your care for others is the _____ of your greatness"; reference standard (Luk. 9:48)

7 Examined into closely; passed through a sieve (Amo. 9:9)

13 Year after leaving Egypt that Aaron died (Num. 33:38)

15 Moment (Luk. 8:44)

17 Hebrews' one allowable permanent worship center in Jerusalem (Exo. 25:8)

18 "It's wonderful to be young! Enjoy every _____ of it! Do all you want to... but realize that you must account to God for everything you do" (Ecc. 11:9)

19 Number of silver coins Judas paid for betraying Jesus (Mat. 26:15)

22 "_____ days later, at the baby's circumcision ceremony, he was named Jesus" (Luk. 2:21)

23 Nothing more than what's specified (Pro. 29:19)

ACROSS

1 Dine (Rev. 3:20; KJV)
4 Midianite king (Num. 31:8)
8 ____-Hamath, Promised Land boundary marker (Num. 34:7)
12 Sin (2 Ch. 33:9; KJV)
13 Midianite general (Jdg. 7:25)
14 Elderly (Deu. 32:7)
15 Untruth (Gen. 3:4)
16 Alienated (Job 19:13; KJV)
18 Donkey (Gen. 16:12)
19 Plus (Gen. 1:1)
20 Resource management (Isa. 29:23)
25 Cultivate (Isa. 5:6)
28 Disregarded (1 Ki. 12:13)
30 Request (Gen. 24:14)
31 Cisterns (1 Ki. 7:38)
32 Shout of disapproval (Job 27:23)
34 Without charge (Gen. 23:11)
35 Sum total (Gen. 1:8)
36 Without help (Isa. 63:5)
38 Attention getter (Mar. 15:32)
39 Folks (Gen. 38:11)
41 What Jesus quieted (Mar. 4:39)
42 Possessed
45 Mediate (Lev. 10:10)
51 Roman three
52 Ascertain (Gen. 45:16)
53 Spoken (Dan. 1:18)
54 Wide-mouthed cooking container (Lev. 2:7)
55 Contributes (Pro. 10:22)
56 Shealtiel's father (Luk. 3:27)
57 Female reference (Gen. 2:23)

DOWN

1 City in Edom (2 Ki. 14:7)
2 "____ son was Bezalel" (1 Ch. 2:20)
3 Now (Mat. 26:53; KJV)
4 Deer (2 Sa. 2:18; KJV)
5 ____ brother, Onan (Gen. 38:8)
6 Wager (2 Ki. 18:23)
7 Sarai's husband (Gen. 11:31)
8 Country (Gen. 2:11)
9 Food from hen (Luk. 11:12)
10 Relative of a hornet (Psa. 118:12)
11 Unusual (Ecc. 8:10)
17 One or another (Gen. 3:1)
21 Mediterranean island (Act. 21:1)
22 Alternative (Gen. 3:3)
23 Babylonian king: abbr. (2 Ki. 24:1)
24 Scent (Joh. 12:3; KJV)
25 Misfortunes (Neh. 9:32)
26 O.T. writer (Rom. 9:25; KJV)
27 ____ out a living
28 District of Babylon (2 Ki. 18:34; KJV)
29 Windstorm (Joh. 6:18)
33 Singular (Gen. 2:24)
34 Suitable (Gen. 49:20)
37 One (Gen. 8:11)
39 Cherished creature (Job 41:5)
40 First Hebrew priest (Exo. 28:1)
41 Honored ones (Gen. 18:3)
43 Father of Rizpah (2 Sa. 21:8)
44 Eat a main meal (2 Sa. 11:11)
45 Triumph cry (Psa. 35:21)
46 Crimson (Exo. 26:14)
47 Not good (Gen. 2:17)
48 "We ____ saved by trusting" (Rom. 8:24)
49 Waterproofing substance (Exo. 2:3)
50 Samuel's appointed guardian (1 Sa. 1:25)

PUZZLE 65

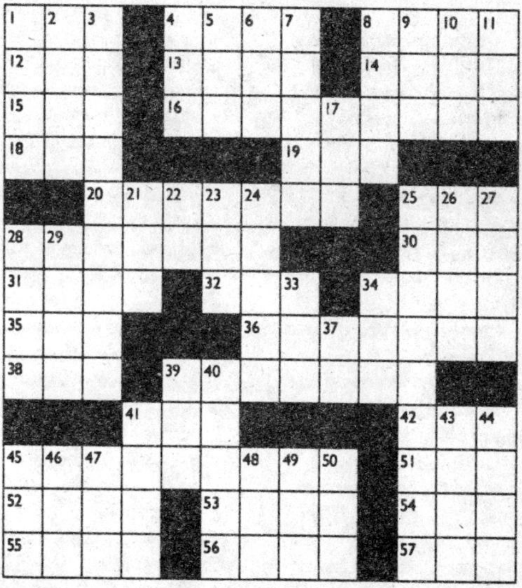

ACROSS

1 Jesus' apostle Simon was also called "The ____" (Act. 1:14)
4 Profane; lacking reverence for sacred matters (Lev. 10:1)
7 "It is destined that men die only ____, and after that comes judgment" (Heb. 9:27)
8 Ruler who exercises absolute power (Eph. 1:21)
9 Killed for one's beliefs (Rev. 16:6)
12 Plead; appeal (Gen. 50:17)
15 River branch in Garden of Eden (Gen. 2:14)
16 Realm of many countries (Ezr. 1:2)
17 "The idols of Babylon, ____ and Nebo, are being hauled away on ox carts" (Isa. 46:1)
19 "God called the light 'daytime,' and the ____ 'nighttime'" (Gen. 1:5)
24 "Here on earth you will have many trials and sorrows; but cheer up, for I have ____ the world" (Joh. 16:33)
25 City where Paul was under house arrest for two years (Act. 28:16, 30)
26 Harsh ruler with absolute power (Rev. 11:7)
27 Mourn; bewail (Isa. 16:9)

DOWN

1 City of David; Jerusalem (2 Sa. 5:7)
2 "The Lord himself will come down from heaven with a mighty shout and with the soul-stirring cry of the ____" (1 Th. 4:16)
3 "Right now God is ready to welcome you. ____ he is ready to save you" (2 Co. 6:2)
4 Laban's relationship to Jacob and Esau (Gen. 28:5)
5 "'This ____,' Laban continued, 'stands between us as a witness of our vows'" (Gen. 31:51)
6 Release from restraint (Eze. 7:3)
10 "The star was called 'Bitterness' because it poisoned a ____ of all the water on the earth" (Rev. 8:11)
11 "Jesus spoke to the ____ within the man and said, 'Come out, you evil spirit'" (Mk. 5:7)
12 "Fire and ____ rained down from heaven and destroyed them all" (Luk. 17:29)
13 Mood of joy and high spirits (Jdg. 15:14)
14 Wound with a pointed weapon (2 Sa. 20:10)
18 Diplomatic messenger (Isa. 37:8)
20 "His unchanging plan has always been to ____ us into his own family" (Eph. 1:5)
21 "Come, ____ before the Lord our Maker, for he is our God" (Psa. 95:6, 7)
22 Judean city given to Caleb (Jos. 15:13)
23 "Since everything around us is going to ____ away, what holy, godly lives we should be living!" (2 Pe. 3:11)

ACROSS

1 "The holy Jerusalem was built on twelve layers of foundation stones _____ with gems"; decorated with a pattern set into a surface (Rev. 21:19)
5 Jeremiah's scribe and secretary (Jer. 36:18)
8 "Don't fail to correct your children; discipline won't hurt them! They won't die if you _____ a stick on them"; implement (Pro. 23:13)
9 "Shine out like _____ lights among people who are crooked and stubborn"; guiding or warning (Phi. 2:15)
10 Seat for riding on horseback (Gen. 31:34)
11 Restaurant's list of food (Est. 2:9)
12 "I have known from _____ days that your will never changes"; first-occurring (Psa. 119:152)
14 Eminent; perceived as better (1 Ch. 4:9)
18 Affecting many persons at one time (2 Ch. 7:13)
20 "Let me tell you how happy God has made me! For he has clothed me with garments of salvation and draped about me the _____ of righteousness"; long, outer garment (Isa. 61:10)
22 Drowsy (Gen. 2:21)
24 Release from restraint (Num. 5:18)
25 Wager (Isa. 36:8)
26 Cling (Act. 15:1)
27 Enclosed with a protective border of shrubs (Mat. 21:33)

DOWN

2 Daughter of one's brother or sister (Gen. 11:29)
3 "I will appoint responsible shepherds to care for them, and they shall not need to be afraid again; all of them shall be _____ for continually"; regarded or watched (Jer. 23:4)
4 Underground prison (Gen. 41:14)
5 Brook in Palestine (1 Sa. 30:9)
6 "You commanded the _____ Sea to divide, forming a dry road across its bottom. Yes, as dry as any desert" (Psa. 106:9)
7 "From: Paul, chosen by God to be Jesus Christ's messenger. To: The faithful Christian brothers— God's people—in the city of _____."
11 Soft, wet earth (Jon. 9:6)
13 "As for the one who conquers, he will have my new Name _____ upon him"; engraved (Rev. 3:12)
15 Pierced with something sharp and pointed (Gen. 41:13)
16 Rude or vulgar (1 Sa. 25:3)
17 "You shall give _____ honor and respect to the elderly, in the fear of God"; expected or proper (Lev. 19:32)
19 "The crowd was amazed. '_____ Jesus is the Messiah!'"; perhaps (Mat. 12:23)
21 "Jehoram had married one of the daughters of Ahab, and his whole life was one constant _____ of doing evil"; spree (2 Ch. 21:6)
23 Before (Joh. 4:49; KJV)

ACROSS

1 "Again Peter ____ it. And immediately a rooster crowed" (Joh. 18:27)
5 "I even found great pleasure in hard work. This pleasure was, indeed, my only reward for all my ____" (Ecc. 2:10)
8 Not private (1 Co. 14:19)
9 "God declares us 'not ____' of offending him if we trust in Jesus Christ" (Rom. 3:24)
10 Beat with a rod or whip (Mk. 10:34)
11 "If it is an ____ —a case in which something is thrown unintentionally, without anger" (Num. 35:22, 23)
12 This number (Mk. 3:14)
14 "No one gets anything until it is ____ that the person who wrote the will is dead" (Heb. 9:16)
16 Carefully worked out plan of action (Gen. 32:20)
19 "God's truth stands ____ like a great rock, and nothing can shake it" (2 Ti. 2:19)
21 "He powerfully refuted all the Jewish arguments in public ____, showing by the Scriptures that Jesus is indeed the Messiah" (Act. 18:28)
22 "A man's poverty is no ____ for twisting justice against him" (Exo. 23:6)
23 "In the book of ____, we are told that the Lord knows full well how the human mind reasons" (1 Co. 3:20)
24 To put forcibly into a position (Psa. 88:6)

DOWN

2 "'With whom will you compare me? Who is my ____?' asks the Holy One" (Isa. 40:25)
3 "It is ____ to take a millstone as a pledge, for it is a tool by which its owner gains his livelihood" (Deu. 24:6)
4 Speak to a person to record (Jer. 36:17)
5 "I will give you the right words and such ____ that none of your opponents will be able to reply!" (Luk. 21:15)
6 "Many people can ____ houses, but only God made everything" (Heb. 3:4)
7 "A very great ____ of aides and servants accompanied the Queen of Sheba" (2 Ch. 9:1)
13 "Do not cooperate with an evil man by affirming on the ____ stand something you know is false" (Exo. 23:1)
14 Return for goods or services (Gen. 42:25)
15 Person charged with law enforcement (Act. 22:26)
17 "All your feverish plans will not ____, for you never ask for help from God" (Isa. 22:11)
18 "The land lies fair as ____ Garden in all its beauty" (Joe. 2:3)
20 Ceases action; stays (2 Ki. 2:15)

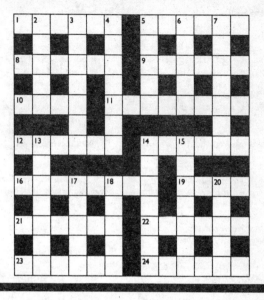

ACROSS

1 Excellent (Isa. 5:12)
5 "God's Messenger is like a blazing fire refining precious metal, and he can ____ the dirtiest garments"; whiten (Mal. 3:2)
8 "Even the birds of the ____ and the fish in the sea will perish" (Zep. 1:3)
9 "God doesn't ____ to the prayers of those who flout the law"; pay attention to (Pro. 28:9)
10 "If your brother is bothered by what you eat, you are not ____ in love if you go ahead and eat it"; behaving (Rom. 14:15)
11 Class or kind (Mk. 2:15)
12 "Forgive us our sins; for we also forgive every one that is ____ to us"; obligated (Luk. 11:4; KJV)
14 "Give me an ____ mind so that I can govern your people well and know the difference between what is right and what is wrong" (1 Ki. 3:9)
17 Discontments aroused by others' possessions or abilities (2 Co. 12:20)
19 Thought (1 Ti. 1:7)
21 "The Lord replies: 'I will be your lawyer; I will plead your case; I will ____ you'"; exact retribution (Jer. 51:36)
23 Man who tested God's will with a fleece (Jdg. 6:39)
24 "At last the king gave the order for Daniel's arrest, and he was taken to the ____ of lions" (Dan. 6:16)
25 Loose head coverings (Rut. 3:15)
26 "Then they will come to their ____ and escape from Satan's trap of slavery to sin"; sound mental capacities (2 Ti. 2:26)

DOWN

2 "The Lord God says: 'I am bringing the people of Israel home from around the world to their own land to ____ them into one nation'"; make a coherent whole (Eze. 37:21, 22)
3 Remotely; outermost (Eze. 46:19)
4 Outlaws; robbers (Luk. 10:30)
5 "When someone becomes a Christian, he becomes a ____ new person inside"; distinctively (2 Co. 5:17)
6 "Stay awake, work hard, and there will be plenty to ____!" (Pro. 20:13)
7 Water container (Gen. 21:19)
13 Unable to get up due to illness (Act. 9:33)
15 City where Jonah preached (Jon. 3:1)
16 Appoints as a task (Gen. 40:4)
18 "If you give to the poor, your ____ will be supplied"; lacks (Pro. 28:27)
20 "Don't store up treasures here on earth where they can ____ away or may be stolen"; gradually wear (Mat. 6:19)
22 "We will have wonderful ____ bodies in heaven, made for us by God himself"; not old (2 Co. 5:1)

ACROSS

1 "The mountains may ____ and the hills disappear, but my kindness shall not leave you"; go away (Isa. 54:10)
5 First O.T. prophetic book
8 Went quickly on foot (Luk. 19:4)
9 "The power of the life-giving Spirit has freed me from the vicious ____ of sin and death"; round (Rom. 8:2)
10 "You have listened to my troubles and have seen the ____ in my soul"; strait (Psa. 31:7)
11 Jacob's son whose descendants became tabernacle workers (Gen. 35:23; Num. 3:6)
12 "Any story sounds true until someone tells the other side and sets the record ____"; correct (Pro. 18:17)
14 "Enjoy the ____ of those who love the Lord" (2 Ti. 2:22)
18 Shape of the moon in its first quarter (Jdg. 8:26)
20 "I have placed my rainbow in the clouds as a ____ of my promise" (Gen. 9:13)
22 "All the world will stand ____ at what I will do for you" (Mic. 7:16)
24 Models or standards of excellence (Psa. 26:3)
25 "Wisdom is its ____ reward, and if you scorn her, you hurt only yourself"; self (Pro. 9:12)
26 "God is not ____. How can he forget your hard work for him?" (Heb. 6:10)
27 "All the rest of the world around us is under ____ power and control"; the devil's (1 Jo. 5:19)

DOWN

2 Banish from one's country (Deu. 28:36)
3 Co-recipient of Paul's letter to Philemon; "a soldier of the cross" (Phm. 1:1, 2)
4 Attempt to overthrow the government (2 Ki. 11:14)
5 Become liable for
6 King Hezekiah's mother (2 Ki. 18:1, 2)
7 Brother of Joab and Asahel; companion of David (1 Sa. 26:6)
11 Site: abbr. (Num. 3:24)
13 Firmly demanding (Act. 21:20)
15 Boat rowers
16 Gains or attains by planned action or effort
17 "Oh, that I could write my plea with an iron ____ in the rock forever"; writing instrument (Job 19:23)
19 Village where King Saul consulted a medium (1 Sa. 28:7)
21 Heights northeast of the Sea of Galilee (Jos. 20:8)
23 Head of one of the seven clans of the tribe of Gad (1 Ch. 5:11, 13)

ACROSS

1 "God says, 'Your _____ came to me at a favorable time, when the doors of welcome were wide open'"; call for help (2 Co. 6:2)

3 Orderly assemblage, such as of troops (1 Ch. 12:38)

9 "Run from sex sin. No other sin _____ the body as this one does"; has an influence (1 Co. 6:18)

11 Jacob's uncle; father of Rachel (Gen. 27:43; 29:16)

12 Inflamed swelling; one of ten plagues on Egypt (Exo. 9:9)

13 For men only, such as a party (Mk. 6:21)

14 "God made the _____ into a woman, and brought her to the man"; curved bone attached to the spine (Gen. 2:22)

16 God's characteristic of showing pity and sharing human sufferings (Exo. 22:27)

18 Woman belonging to a religious order

20 Fall in drops (Amo. 9:13)

21 Move in leaps and steps (Psa. 29:5)

24 Body part performing a specific function (Lev. 1:9)

25 Put a riding seat on an animal (Gen. 22:3)

26 "If ye _____ in me, and my words _____ in you, ye shall ask what ye will, and it shall be done unto you"; remain or dwell in (Joh. 15:7; KJV)

27 "The living beings darted to and _____, swift as lightning"; away (Eze. 1:14)

DOWN

2 "May my spoken words and unspoken thoughts be pleasing even to you, O Lord my _____ and my Redeemer"; solid support (Psa. 19:14)

4 "When we teachers of _____, who should know better, do wrong, our punishment will be greater than it would be for others"; organized system of faith and worship (Jam. 3:1)

5 Brownish-yellow color (Eze. 8:2)

6 "John saw Jesus coming toward him and said, 'Look! There is the _____ of God who takes away the world's sin'"; young sheep (Joh. 1:29)

7 Assert positively (Exo. 23:1)

8 Give power to (1 Ti. 1:12; KJV)

10 "The Lord _____ the thirsty soul and fills the hungry soul with good"; provides all that's needed (Psa. 107:9)

15 "Your body will die because of sin; but your spirit will live, for Christ has _____ it"; freed from penalty (Rom. 8:10)

16 Artillery to propel large balls (Isa. 65:23)

17 Basic, soluble mineral salt (Deu. 29:23)

19 Arid region in southern Palestine (Gen. 20:1)

22 "The boy became so hungry that even the _____ he was feeding the swine looked good to him"; fruit husks that split open (Luk. 15:16)

23 Smell (Num. 28:6)

142

ACROSS

1 "You furnish lovely music at your grand parties; the orchestras are _____! But for the Lord you have no thought or care"; outstanding (Isa. 5:12)

5 Long-haired (Dan. 8:21)

8 "_____ fall short of God's glorious ideal"; everyone (Rom. 3:23)

9 Shield or hide (Exo. 40:21)

10 As much as one can carry with one arm (Act. 28:3)

11 "No one anywhere can ever _____ in the presence of God. For it is from God alone that you have your life through Christ Jesus"; boast (1 Co. 1:29, 30)

12 Maximum or extreme (Eze. 27:10)

14 "I am eighty years old today, and life has lost its excitement. Food and wine are no longer tasty, and _____ is not much fun"; diversion (2 Sa. 19:35)

18 Largest fabric to catch wind and propel a boat (Act. 27:40; KJV)

20 Behind or back (Mat. 26:58)

22 "A time to tear; A time to _____"; fix (Ecc. 3:7)

24 Eighteen-inch lengths (Exo. 25:10; KJV)

25 "With Rachel's last breath (for she died) she named him 'Ben_____' ('Son of my sorrow')" (Gen. 35:18)

26 "To _____ this honor and renown you must be a holy people to the Lord your God, as he requires"; achieve (Deu. 26:19)

27 Ditch (1 Ki. 18:32)

DOWN

2 Open sore (Lev. 13:10)

3 "I am like an _____ tree, yielding my fruit to you throughout the year. My mercies never fail"; having foliage that doesn't change color (Hos. 14:8)

4 Ceremonial dinner (Mat. 22:3)

5 "Do not _____ your testimony in favor of a man just because he is poor"; present with a special viewpoint (Exo. 23:3)

6 "If your _____ is to enjoy the evil pleasure of the unsaved world, you cannot also be a friend of God"; goal (Jam. 4:4)

7 One who eats to excess (Mat. 11:19)

11 "They swarm around me like _____"; stinging insect: sing. (Psa. 118:12)

13 Worth remembering; noteworthy

15 Closest (2 Sa. 17:13)

16 Not lawful

17 "Moses' mother made a little boat from papyrus reeds, waterproofed it with _____, put the baby in it, and laid it among the reeds along the river's edge" (Exo. 2:3)

19 Miriam's brother (Exo. 15:20)

21 "It is better to live in a corner of an _____ than in a beautiful home with a cranky, quarrelsome woman"; space just below roof (Pro. 25:24)

23 A son of Ithran (1 Ch. 7:38)

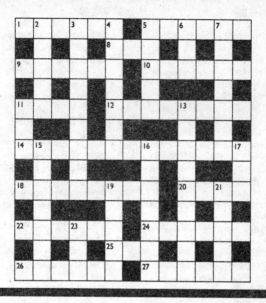

ACROSS

1 Contemptible, base people (Psa. 35:15; KJV)
5 Of the 12 Hebrew spies, only Joshua and _____ were allowed to enter the Promised Land (Num. 14:38)
8 "Don't envy the wicked. Don't _____ his riches"; desire enviably (Pro. 24:19)
9 "The Prince of the bottomless pit whose name in Hebrew is _____, and in Greek, Apollyon [and in English, the Destroyer]" (Rev. 9:11)
10 Warned; informed beforehand (Jdg. 16:2)
12 "Obey your father and your mother, for their advice is a _____ of light directed into the dark corners of your mind to warn you of danger and to give you a good life"; ray (Pro. 6:20, 23)
16 "God gave Paul the power to do unusual miracles, so that even when his _____ or parts of his clothing were placed upon sick people, they were healed"; small pieces of cloth (Act. 19:11, 12)
18 "A happy _____ means a glad heart"; countenance (Pro. 15:13)
20 "During the night some of Paul's converts let him down in a basket through an _____ in the city wall"; gap (Act. 9:25)
23 Welcome hug (Pro. 5:19)
24 Recurring round of events
25 Move rhythmically to music (Sg. 6:13)
26 "You constantly _____ the hunger and thirst of every living thing"; fulfill the desires or needs of (Psa. 145:16)

DOWN

1 "The stone rejected by the builders has now become the capstone of the _____"; top part of a doorway (Psa. 118:22)
2 Light spear (Job 39:23)
3 Sever with a sharp edge (Exo. 35:33)
4 "The land is mine, so you may not sell it permanently. You are merely my tenants and _____"; farmers who work another's land for produce (Lev. 25:23)
5 "As the _____ is in the potter's hand, so are you in my hand"; moist soil for shaping (Jer. 18:6)
6 Shelflike projection (Exo. 27:5)
7 Word meaning "son" in Hebrew (Gen. 35:18)
11 Long-handled garden tool with a row of projecting teeth at one end
13 "I've blotted out your sins; they are gone like morning _____ at noon"; visible water vapor (Isa. 44:22)
14 Head cook (1 Sa. 9:23)
15 Part of face below mouth (Lev. 13:29)
17 Castrated men (2 Ki. 9:32)
19 Living compartment on a ship (Eze. 27:6)
21 Infant (Exo. 2:6; KJV)
22 Large group (Est. 2:19)
23 "Proud men _____ in shame, but the meek become wise"; finish (Pro. 11:2)
24 Small, portable bed

ACROSS

1 "May God our Father and the Lord Jesus Christ mightily _____ each one of you and give you peace" (2 Co. 1:2)

4 Instructive talk (Act. 19:9)

8 Sound of a pigeon

9 Bathsheba's first husband (2 Sa. 11:3)

10 Covering; disguising (Psa. 18:11)

11 Those who inform on others (1 Ti. 5:13; KJV)

12 "The Lord is my strength, my _____, and my salvation" (Exo. 15:2)

14 "In every battle you will need faith as your shield to stop the _____ arrows aimed at you by Satan"; burning (Eph. 6:16)

16 "What a _____ yes, how stupid!—to decide before knowing the facts" (Pro. 18:13)

20 "God has planted them like strong and graceful _____ for his own glory" (Isa. 61:3)

21 "Not until the heavens can be measured and the foundations of the earth _____, will I consider casting them away forever for their sins" (Jer. 31:37)

24 Brief look (Act. 1:10)

25 Hezekiah made a _____ of dried figs and spred it on his boil (2 Ki. 20:7)

26 Drink in small quantities (Eze. 12:19)

27 Uzziah produced _____ of war; invented by brilliant men (2 Ch. 26:15)

28 Haman asked the king to _____ a decree that the Jews be destroyed (Est. 3:9)

DOWN

1 "Only a fool _____ out everything he knows; that only leads to sorrow and trouble"; utters suddenly (Pro. 10:14)

2 "What can you point to that is new? How do you know it didn't _____ long ages ago?; be (Ecc. 1:10)

3 "God gives wise men their wisdom and _____ their intelligence"; learned people (Dan. 2:21)

4 Sexual partners (Pro. 7:11)

5 "We toss the _____, but it is the Lord who controls its decision"; piece of metal used as currency (Pro. 16:33)

6 "The Lord himself will seat them and put on a waiter's _____ and serve them as they sit and eat!" (Luk. 12:37)

7 Bring into battle contact (1 Ch. 19:10)

13 City to which Paul wrote, "Always be full of joy in the Lord; I say it again, rejoice!"

15 Hint or idea

17 "If you want a happy, good life, keep control of your _____, and guard your lips from telling lies" (1 Pe. 3:10)

18 Amount left over (Gen. 41:35)

19 Remain loyal; stick fast (Act. 15:1)

22 "The spirit of Elijah _____ upon Elisha"; lies fixed upon (2 Ki. 2:15)

23 "_____ my eyes to see wonderful things in your Word"; remove obstructions from (Psa. 119:18)

SOLUTIONS

Puzzle 1, Page 3

Puzzle 2, Page 5

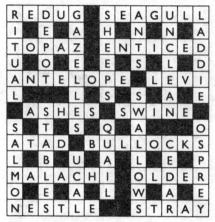

Puzzle 3, Page 7

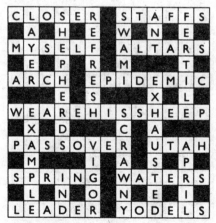

Puzzle 4, Page 9

Puzzle 5, Page 11

Puzzle 6, Page 13

154

Puzzle 7, Page 15

Puzzle 8, Page 17

Puzzle 7, Page 15

Puzzle 8, Page 17

Puzzle 9, Page 19

Puzzle 10, Page 21

156

```
C A S A B A   P E N I E L
A N T H E M   E Q U A T E
U N R U L Y   R U B T H E
D U O M O     F A I R E R
A L L A N D   E L A I N E
D I L I G E N C E   C E D
      S E T
C R T   E P H E S I A N S
A H A S A I   D A C R O N
L Y I N G S     M E N T A
E M P A L E   D A C O I T
S E A R E R   B R A N C H
A R N E S S   L A P S E S
```

Puzzle 11, Page 23

```
S Y R I A   C R E T A N S
U   E   M   Y   X   R   A
N E C H O   R E P H A I M
D   T   R   E   O   M   S
A R A B I A N S   H A L O N
Y       T   E   B   I   N
  M E D E S   E R E C H
M   D   S   G   A       E
O D O R   A R A M E A N S
S   M   T   E   B   R   T
A B I L E N E   L Y N C H
I   T   M   K   E   O   E
C A E S A R S   S E N I R
```

Puzzle 12, Page 25

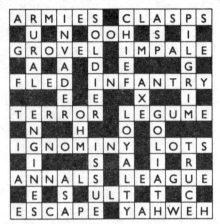

Puzzle 13, Page 27

A	R	M	I	E	S		C	L	A	S	P	S
	U		N		O	O	H		S		I	
G	R	O	V	E	L		I	M	P	A	L	E
	A		A		D		E				G	
F	L	E	D		I	N	F	A	N	T	R	Y
			E		E		X				I	
T	E	R	R	O	R		L	E	G	U	M	E
	N		H				O		O			
I	G	N	O	M	I	N	Y		L	O	T	S
	I			S		A		I		R		
A	N	N	A	L	S		L	E	A	G	U	E
	E		S		U	L	T		T		C	
E	S	C	A	P	E		Y	A	H	W	E	H

Puzzle 13, Page 27

Puzzle 14, Page 29

B	E	H	A	L	F		A	R	A	B	A	H
	A		D		R	O	B		H		R	
S	T	A	D	I	A		I	S	A	I	A	H
	E		I		M		H				M	
K	N	I	T		E	D	U	C	A	T	E	D
			I		U			B			A	
A	C	C	O	M	P	L	I	S	H	I	N	G
	A		N				N		O			
A	P	O	S	T	L	E	S		R	A	G	E
	A				E		T		R		E	
A	B	L	A	Z	E		A	G	E	N	C	Y
	L		M		K	I	N		N		K	
B	E	G	I	N	S		T	A	T	T	O	O

Puzzle 14, Page 29

158

Puzzle 15, Page 31

Puzzle 16, Page 33

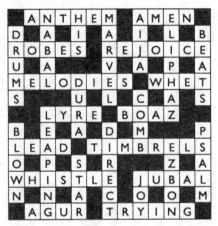

Puzzle 17, Page 35

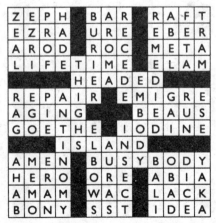

Puzzle 18, Page 37

Puzzle 19, Page 39

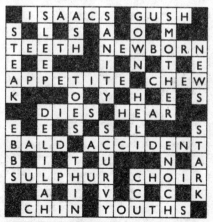

Puzzle 20, Page 41

Puzzle 21, Page 43

Puzzle 22, Page 45

162

Puzzle 23, Page 47

Grid 1 (Puzzle 23):

A	L	T	A	R	S		C	H	A	R	M	S
	I		R		U	R	I		L		A	
K	N	O	C	K	S		V	I	L	E	L	Y
	E		H		T		I				A	
A	N	T	I		A	L	L	I	A	N	C	E
			P		L				B		H	
C	O	M	P	A	N	I	O	N	S	H	I	P
	B		U		V			T				
C	A	P	S	T	O	N	E		A	D	D	S
	D			A			R		I		A	
B	I	R	T	H	S		F	I	N	I	N	G
	A		E		E	V	E		E		C	
C	H	E	A	T	S		D	O	D	G	E	D

Puzzle 24, Page 49

Grid 2 (Puzzle 24):

L	A	U	G	H	E	D		D	O	Z	E	N
I		N		I		I	R	A		U		O
F	R	I	N	G	E	S		U	Z	Z	I	A
E		F		H		C		G		I		H
	T	Y	P	E		S	C	H	E	M	E	S
	R		S			T				E	N	
B	U	R	N	T	O	F	F	E	R	I	N	G
	E		R			R		R		U		
P	R	I	V	A	C	Y		I	L	A	I	
A		R		N		E		N		L		O
C	R	A	C	K		A	L	L	O	T	E	D
K		Q		E	R	S		A		A		D
S	H	I	E	D		T	H	W	A	R	T	S

Puzzle 24, Page 49

163

Puzzle 25, Page 51

Puzzle 26, Page 53

164

Puzzle 27, Page 55

Puzzle 28, Page 57

Puzzle 29, Page 59

Puzzle 30, Page 61

Puzzle 31, Page 63

Puzzle 32, Page 65

Puzzle 33, Page 67

Across/Down grid:

```
C H R I S T   P R E A C H
  O   C   H   A   A   O
I N V O K E   N A T U R E
  O   N   U   I   E   I
A R N I   D O C T R I N E
      U   A           T
P A T M O S   W O R T H Y
  B       A   E
M I R A C L E S   V O W S
  L   R   I   H   I   I
R I M M O N   I N V E S T
  T   O   U   N   E   E
C Y P R U S   G A D A R A
```

Puzzle 34, Page 69

```
C H A P E L   S C O F F S
  U   R   A M I   F   R
E R R A N D   N A T H A N
  R   Y   D   C       N
T Y R E   E L E V E N T H
      R   R       L   I
S E L F A S S U R A N C E
  D   U       N   B
B I L L O W E D   O N C E
  F       O   E   R   R
D I S A R M   R E A D E R
  E   D   B E G   T   T
O D I O U S   O B E Y E D
```

Puzzle 35, Page 71

Puzzle 36, Page 73

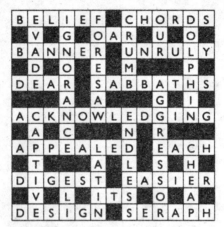

Puzzle 37, Page 75

Puzzle 38, Page 77

Puzzle 39, Page 79

Puzzle 40, Page 81

Puzzle 41, Page 83

Puzzle 42, Page 85

Puzzle 43, Page 87

Puzzle 44, Page 89

Puzzle 45, Page 91

Puzzle 46, Page 93

174

Puzzle 47, Page 95

Puzzle 48, Page 97

Puzzle 49, Page 99

Puzzle 50, Page 101

Puzzle 51, Page 103

Puzzle 52, Page 105

Puzzle 53, Page 107

Puzzle 54, Page 109

Puzzle 55, Page 111

The grid for Puzzle 55 reads:

P	E	T	S		I	D	D	O		O	P	P
A	C	R	O		S	E	E	D		N	E	R
C	O	U	P		A	B	E	D	N	E	G	O
E	L	E	A	Z	A	R		S	O	S		
		T	A	C	I	T		W	I	S	P	
L	A	S	E	R		S	I	S		M	E	A
A	B	I	R	A	M		S	A	M	U	E	L
M	A	L		H	E	N		T	A	S	K	S
A	D	V	T		N	E	B	A	T			
		A	U	G		P	O	N	T	I	U	S
S	Y	N	T	Y	C	H	E		H	O	R	A
I	O	U		P	E	E	R		E	W	E	S
B	U	S		S	A	W	S		W	A	Y	S

Puzzle 56, Page 113

The grid for Puzzle 56 reads:

G	E	M		E	A	C	H		A	G	A	G
A	M	A		B	I	L	E		B	A	D	E
Z	I	P	P	O	R	A	H		I	D	D	O
A	R	S	O	N		D	E	A	D			
			A	Y	E		H	A	B	I	T	
D	I	S	C		Z	I	O	N		A	L	E
A	D	A	H		E	N	D		C	L	A	N
R	E	G		T	R	A	D		L	E	I	S
A	S	A	P	H			S	B	A			
		L	E	A	F		L	I	A	R	S	
Z	I	Z	A		N	E	H	E	M	I	A	H
A	T	I	C		T	A	O	S		A	C	A
G	A	P	E		S	L	I	T		H	A	D

179

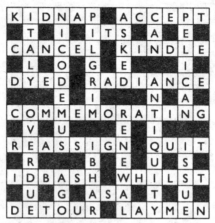

Puzzle 57, Page 115

Puzzle 58, Page 117

Puzzle 59, Page 119

Puzzle 60, Page 121

Puzzle 61, Page 123

Puzzle 62, Page 125

```
E G G S   W A D E   B R O
R I O T   O A R S   A A B
A S E R   R A I S I N G S
S T R U C K   E A T E S T
    T A M   D Y E
O C T   B E D   S M A L L
G A A L   N B A   S C A B
S T E E D   A R D   A B S
    V A L   R E A
S E R E N E   A L T E R S
A D U L T E R Y   O B E Y
D A G   E C C E   N A I N
A M A   S H A D   E L S E
```

Puzzle 63, Page 127

```
T R A I N   C O L U M N S
I   M   I L L   I   E   I
T H O R N   O N E H A L F
H   N   E   V   S   S   T
E I G H T E E N   J U N E
S       E   N   F   R   D
  W I V E S   D O Z E N
T   N   N   M   R       T
E A S Y   F I F T I E T H
M   T   M   N   I   I   I
P L A T E A U   E A G E R
L   N   R   T A T   H   T
E X T R E M E   H O T L Y
```

Puzzle 64, Page 129

Puzzle 65, Page 131

Puzzle 66, Page 133

Puzzle 67, Page 135

Puzzle 68, Page 137

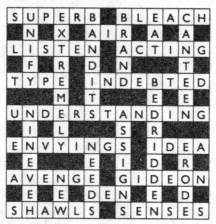

Puzzle 69, Page 139

Puzzle 70, Page 141